Stories of a Small Boonton USA

By
Lloyd and Terry Charlton

Iron Works painted by Bob Bogue

Date of Publication of this Book

December 2010

Hi, I'm Terry Crespo Charlton, Lloyd's wife of 10 years. My roots are in Brooklyn, New York where I grew up in an immigrant community that has long ago disappeared. Needless to say, I was awed when I came to live in Boonton and found so many of my husband's friends still living nearby

In 2009, our local Historical Society was looking for a volunteer to interview some of Boonton's senior citizens and to document their stories in video. Lloyd and I dreamed up some questions and set out on the adventure. Our fantasy is that in 100 years from now someone will discover these interviews and get to meet the actual citizens of Boonton who were born in the 1920s and 1930s.

I dedicate this book to my children, Carol, Jim, Ray and Joe Crespo, who have always been my best cheerleaders! I thank Lloyd for his collaboration on the book. He is my husband, my best friend and my dearest love.

Hi. I'm Lloyd Charlton. My great grandfather, Hon. Joshua Salmon, was born in Mt. Olive and came to Boonton as a young man. He became an attorney, fire chief and a mayor here, and became a U.S. Congressman in 1898. This is my story about Boonton as I knew it – from when I was born in the late 1920s until today. This book is also dedicated to my children and grandchildren:

Angelo and Nancy Charlton Questa and grandsons Anthony and Nick
Bill and Adrienne Burke Charlton and granddaughters Bridget and Jackie
Art and Susan Leitzke Charlton and grandsons John and Joshua

I am writing this for my children so they can remember all the stories I've told them about growing up in Boonton. Terry has been the inspiration for writing this book – and I thank her 'muchly.' Without her, I'd still be on page 5!

The front cover of this book is a painting done by my old friend, Bob Bogue. This painting was featured in the book I published in January 2009 called *"The Artistry of BOB BOGUE."*

STORIES OF A SMALL TOWN
BOONTON USA

By Lloyd and Terry Charlton

This book is available at:

http://www.amazon.com

or

Lloyd & Terry Charlton c/o
Boonton Historical Society
210 Main Street
Boonton NJ 07005
www.boonton.org

or

Email: terrycharlton@optonline.net

Dated: December 2010

List of Participants
to the Historical Society Archive Program

From October 2009 to October 2010, Lloyd and Terry Charlton videotaped interviews with the following people who grew up in Boonton. The people interviewed ranged in age from 70 to a senior citizen who is now 106 years old.

After the interview, Terry wrote a short essay and gave the essay to each participant as a 'thank you.' Copies of those essays are included in this book.

The actual videotaped interviews are being archived at the Boonton Historical Society Museum and we hope in 100 years when people ask - "What were the people who lived in Boonton like?" – They will find video and copies of the interviews in the Museum archives.

ALPHABETICALLY SPEAKING

- Adams, Gilda DeFiore
- Ammann (see Durrer)
- Austin, Edna Martin

- Bacchetta, Al & Edith Bonanni
- Bandura, Betty Sikora
- Banks, Bobby
- Bednar, B./ D.Bonanni \B. Tredway
- Birch, Bill
- Bogue, Bob and Lynn
- Bolcar, Stephen
- Bonanni, Danny (see Bednar)

- Carman, Mary Leva
- Cascella, Ernestine Prevost
- Charlton Lloyd (see Estler)
- Charlton, Robert
- Condon, Al and Grace Fanning
-

  De Eduardo, Marie Siano
- Dunn, Julia
- Durrer, Margo Ammann

- Estler, Don with Lloyd Charlton
- Franchi, Gladys Bertell
- Gibian, Fran Smith

- Halstead, Ruth Doland
- Heaton, Alice Charlton

- Hezlitt, George and Dot
- Higgins, Eleanor
- Hornick, Doris Borgstrom

- Ludwig, Fred

- Marshall, Charlie
- McCormick, Gloria Weiser
- McGlone, Jim
-
- Nikel, Bill
-
- Osterhoudt, Ann Barnish

- Perry, Asperina ("Dixie") Croce

- Reeves, Ann Apgar
- Reeves, Harry

- Scerbo, Lucille Hopkins
- Scozzafava, Tony
- Strelec, Joe

- Tredway, Bill (see Bednar)

- Werner, Paul
- Wiswall, Frank &
     Mae Beiermeister Wiswall

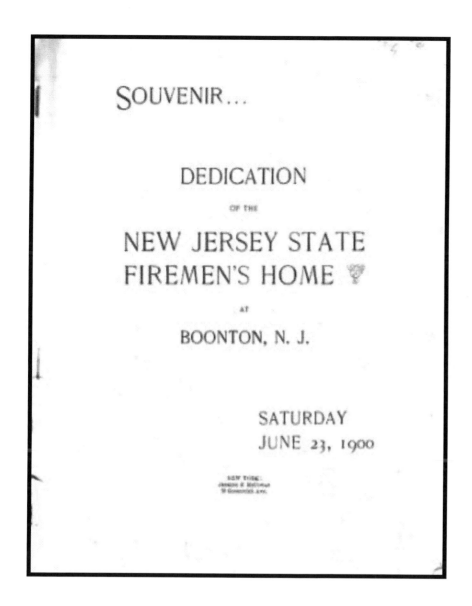

SOUVENIR...

DEDICATION

OF THE

NEW JERSEY STATE
FIREMEN'S HOME ♥

AT

BOONTON, N. J.

SATURDAY
JUNE 23, 1900

I am borrowing a few stories and photographs from the book featured above. It is the *DEDICATION OF THE NEW JERSEY STATE FIREMEN'S HOME June 21, 1900,* the "*Dedication Souvenir.*" It explains that in the 1750s David Ogden was deeded the land in what is now called Boonton.

It indicates that Boonton might have been named for Thomas Boone who was appointed by the King of England as Governor of the Province of New Jersey during the years 1760 to 1762. The town's name was originally spelled "Boone town."

The *Dedication Souvenir* indicated that: "In 1800, Old Boonton had its own church, school-house, post-office, dwelling houses, rolling mill, sawmill, potash factory, nail mill, grist mill and blacksmith shop."

The Iron Works of Old Boonton were among the earliest ever erected in America. Raw materials and finished products were first transported to and from the mills on horseback. Later, with the construction of the Morris Canal reaching from the Delaware River to the Hudson River, materials and products could be transported more readily. The *Dedication Souvenir* proudly stated that, "Japan, China and South America received the products of the Boonton Iron Works." In 1906 a huge fire ended the Iron Works in Boonton.

By the 1830s the New Jersey Iron Works was established in "Boonton Falls." In the *Dedication Souvenir* some important names appeared:

*   Manager Iron Works, Mr. Wm. G. Lathrop (his home is now the Firemen's Home)
*   The Nail Factory, Mr. James Holmes (his home is now Boonton's Library)
*   The Blast Furnace, Mr. George Jenkins
*   The Rolling Mill, Mr. Philip Wootton

Other distinguished men mentioned in the *Dedication Souvenir* include:

*   Hon. Joshua Salmon, a Boonton resident and attorney, who was elected to Congress in 1898 and served until his death in 1902. He was Lloyd's great grandfather.

*   John Hill served in Congress from 1867 to 1873, and again in 1880. He was the father of the popular postal card and the grammar school was dedicated in his memory.

By the turn of the century the factories and rolling mill were things of the past.

By 1903 'Old' Boonton was submerged to create the Jersey City Reservoir.

Some of the men who appeared in the 1900 Dedication Souvenir were shown with photos of their homes

Hon. Joshua Salmon

Lloyd's great grandfather died suddenly in 1902 while serving in the House of Representatives. Many of the stores in Boonton closed in his honor and the Congressmen from D.C. who came to Boonton were impressed by the turnout of the Fire Department at the church service.

PUBLIC LIBRARY AND READING ROOM.

James Holmes

Among the many achievements, he was sent as a delegate to the State Convention and he was very active in community life, even giving his home with $10,000 to the town for its first library.

William Lathrop

Boonton's first Mayor, Judge Lathrop built his home in the late 1800s.

It is now used as the New Jersey State Firemen's Home.

John Hill

A Congressman and Post Master, a grammar school was named for him -

"The John Hill School"

Gov. Foster Voorhees

GOVERNOR FOSTER M. VOORHEES.

Here are some of the men who appeared in the 1900 Dedication Souvenir Book.

Philip Wootton

PHILIP WOOTTON

John Maxfield

JOHN MAXFIELD.

Thomas Capstick

THOMAS CAPSTICK.

John Capstick, Jr.

JOHN CAPSTICK, JR.

Chief John Dunn

SECOND ASSISTANT CHIEF JOHN C. DUNN

Paul Voorhees

John Kanouse

John L. Kanouse

8

William Meadowcroft

In 1910, William H. Meadowcroft, Esq. became a secretary to Thomas Edison and worked for him for many years. He lived in Boonton.

Home of William Meadowcroft

Jimmy Doolittle

General James H. Doolittle
**   "Jimmy" – born in 1896 and died in 1993**

Airplane photo below taken at Aircraft Radio Corporation Airdrome, Boonton Township, NJ

Jimmy was NOT a Boonton resident but I include him in this book because he is an American aviation pioneer. His most important contribution was to aeronautical technology. He was a familiar personality at Aircraft Radio (Boonton, NJ) and ARC personnel installed Jimmy's special receiver and radio gear.

General Doolittle is credited with the first ever airplane flight strictly done by instruments. The cockpit of his biplane was covered completely so that he could not see outside and he took off from the airstrip at Aircraft Radio Corp. in Boonton Township, flew around and returned to land safely strictly by instruments. He also led the United States' first air raid on Tokyo, Japan in World War II.

Othmar Ammann

A Swiss-born civil engineer specializing in long span bridges. Othmar Ammann settled in Boonton's Park section. His name is synonymous with the George Washington Bridge, but he also designed the Goethals Bridge, Bayonne Bridge, Verrazano-Narrows Bridge, Outerbridge Crossing, Triborough, Delaware Memorial, Bronx-Whitestone and many others.

George Washington Bridge

Othmar Ammann

Bayonne Bridge

Verrazano-Narrows Bridge

Othmar Ammann

A Swiss-born civil engineer specializing in long span bridges, Othmar Ammann settled in Boonton's Park section and Lloyd used to deliver mail to his home on Rockaway Street.

Othmar Ammann Bridge

In August 2005, Othmar Ammann's daughter, Margot Ammann Durrer, M.D., arrived with other Boonton dignitaries (riding on a fire truck) to dedicate this newly constructed bridge to Boonton's famous resident.

Charles Hopkins

Building to the left was used by the Underground Railroad.

Lucille Hopkins Scerbo said:
"My grandfather, Charles Hopkins, took a wagon and transported the runaway slaves from the Boonton Underground Railroad Hotel owned by his father to Butler, NJ."

During the Civil War Charles volunteered in the Union Army and was wounded in action several times.
He was taken prisoner and held in the infamous Andersonville prison. After the war the Union prisoners were taken to the train station to be transported back to the North.

Charles was left behind because he was so ill but he was so determined to live that he crawled to the train station.

RESIDENCE OF CHIEF CHARLES F. HOPKINS.

At Boonton's Town Hall a separate monument is dedicated to Charles Hopkins. Charles Hopkins was awarded the Medal of Honor for his bravery in the Civil War. The medal reads:

"Distinguished conduct in action at the Battle of Gaines Mills Virginia June 27, 1862 when he voluntarily carried a wounded comrade under heavy fire to a place of safety and, though twice wounded in the act, he continued in action until again severely wounded."

Postcards of the Canal
& the Iron Works!
These photos came from Joe Strelec's website
www.boontonpostcards.com

Drinking Fountain

Canal 1900 Iron Works

Familiar Scenes in Boonton

Photo 1
Pre-Revolutionary
Jacob Kanouse Homestead
Oldest Frame Dwelling in Township

The four-story plant built by Pelgram and Meyer on Monroe and Lincoln Streets in Boonton employed 500 people until it shut in 1927.

Silk Factory – closed in 1927; it later became the Boonton Handbag Factory and is now Packard Industries.

Kanouse House –Pre Revolutionary War

BUSINESS SECTION, BOONTON N J

Boonton Business District

Park House (now Michelangelo Rest.)

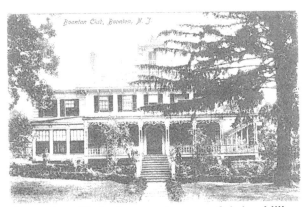

Boonton Club, former home of John Hill

Familiar Scenes in Town

Whelan's Drug Store Main Street and William Street

The Gazebo on Main Street

William Street near Cedar Street

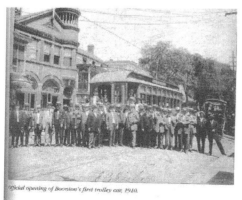

Official opening of trolley in 1910

Picture of Strauss Store and Marcello

Familiar Scenes in Town

Camp Kenilworth, Boonton above –
The Equitable Life Ins. Co. below

"Camp Kenilworth" (above right) became the Equitable Life building, and during the War years when travel was curtailed, Equitable would offer a summer vacation in Boonton for its female employees.

This building stands on Powerville Road at the facility currently called Merry Heart Assisted Living.

Elks Club

Harmony Fire Engine Co.

Familiar Scenes in Town

Laurie Shop

Newberry's

Tucker's & Lehman's

Bob's Men's Shop/Don's Sandwich

Lee's Shoes

Frankels

Familiar Scenes in Town

The Dam, Boonton, N.J.

If you look closely, you can see two "outhouses" in the upper right.

Here is Bob Bogue's painting of the Royal Scarlet Grocery
located in the Brady Building – the same location (without outhouses).

Familiar Scenes in Town

Harmony Drum Corps
Someone guessed this photo was taken around 1920.

Taken in late 1990s

Taken around 2000

Familiar Scenes in Town

Heavenly Temptations on Main Street –
coffee cup filled with snow on a "snowy day"

$9,500
This Beautiful Two Family Duplex House

WITH FIVE GARAGES

New Hot Water Oil Heating Plant

Five Rooms Each Half of Duplex   All City Improvements

IN BUSINESS ZONE

Close to School and Railroad Station

PROGRAM LISTINGS FOR
W M T R
1250 ON THE DIAL
NEWS EVERY HOUR ON THE HOUR

MONDAY through FRIDAY

A newspaper ad in 1949!

Stories of a Small Town – Boonton USA
By
Lloyd and Terry Charlton

DECEMBER 2010

Dear Al and Grace Condon from your old friends from Boonton,

On the occasion of your 60th wedding anniversary, and with congratulations for bringing up such loving children who are giving you this party, we thought it would be fun to write an essay and share with you some of the stories that we've heard about Boonton since we have been interviewing seniors for the Historical Society 'archive' program.

It was 1993 when Lloyd's beautiful wife Ann Pulsinelli Charlton lost her battle with cancer. They had been happily married for 38 years, and 1993 was a time of great sorrow.

So it came as a surprise when, five years later, we met and we fell in love. We were married in 2000.

It was another surprise when the Historical Society asked for volunteers to interview senior citizens who grew up in Boonton and when we tried to do interviews, we found we liked to do them. We have accumulated lots of information about what growing up was like for people born in the 1920s and 1930s. Since you grew up in Boonton, we thought you'd enjoy reminiscing with us.

We grew up during the Great Depression when every family was experiencing financial hardship. As our friend Ernestine Cascella said, "We couldn't paint or remodel the house but my grandmother said, 'If you have a good table, that is the most important thing,' so we always had good food on the table.'"

We were taught all through the 1920s and 1930s "never to waste anything." We continued "never to waste anything" all through the War years when many staples were rationed or hard to come by.

We entered adolescence at the beginning of World War II and we volunteered or were drafted into the military to defend our country. Being in World War II made us grow up very quickly. Some Boonton friends died fighting for our country and for us.

During WWII, people proudly put a flag with a blue star in their front window so everyone in town knew if a family member was serving in the military. If a Gold Star was displayed in a front window, it indicated that a soldier had died in the line of duty defending his country.

It was a Sunday afternoon on December 7, 1941 and lots of people were at the Boonton High School field watching the local semi-pro football team, the Panthers, play football. Bill Bednar was watching the game and his friend came by and said to Bill, "We are at war." To which Bill replied, "What did I ever do to you?" Then an announcement was made over the loudspeaker that Pearl Harbor had been bombed.

I'd like to tell you a few stories we learned from the people we interviewed who were actually in action during WWII.

A FEW STORIES ABOUT WORLD WAR II

Lucille Hopkins Scerbo and her family suffered the loss of her brother, Jody Hopkins, age 23. He was a paratrooper during WWII and he was killed in the Battle of the Bulge and buried in Luxemburg. At the Memorial Day service in Boonton held at the Town Hall each year we honor Jody Hopkins' memory by reading his name along with all the other Boonton servicemen who have died defending our country.

Bill Bednar talked about being in the Marine Corps in Guam. "It was the worst experience of my life going down the ship's ladder. They schooled us for two or three days not to grab the ropes by holding the ladder steps. We had to hold them from the outside so no one above would step on our hands with their boots as they descended. We were wearing a full pack on our back, and wearing a helmet and I knew we were going to drown if we fell off the ladder. I was so glad to get inside that boat!! We were sent to Guam to train for the invasion of Japan." Bill believes there would have been catastrophic losses of American lives had we invaded the Islands of Japan, and that dropping the atomic bomb was necessary. For being willing to fight for your country, we thank you Bill.

Frank Wiswall remembers that there was a period before the War when a person could sign up for one year in the military. His time was nearly up and Frank was ready to be discharged in 1941 when the Japanese dropped bombs on Pearl Harbor so instead of a year of service, Frank served 6 years.

Frank flew as a bombardier on 25 missions (the maximum allowed) over Germany and he earned the Distinguished Flying Cross and an Air Medal four times with three clusters. Then in 2010 the French government awarded him the "French Legion of Honor." Frank was elected to the "Boonton High School Wall of Fame" in August 2010. For your incredible bravery, thank you, Frank.

Another War hero we interviewed was Steve Bolcar. He said on the day he arrived in Tibenhem, UK, on September 27, 1944, he was told that of the 39 B24 planes that had left Tibenhem for Kassell, Germany that day, only 12 aircraft came back.

Steve told us, "We had the most devastating losses of the 8th Air Force Squadron." The French Croix de Guerre (its highest honor) was awarded to the 445th Bomb Group, of which Steve was a part.

On February 24, 1945, when Sergeant Steven Bolcar was working as a gunner on a mission, the aircraft ran into trouble. Shortly after takeoff, Steve reported to the pilot that engine #1 started to spew fire and then began to blaze. The pilot shut down the engine immediately and decided to return to the airfield, but at the last minute he was instructed not to land because of the 20 napalm bombs on board the aircraft.

The plane few low enough to touch treetops while trying to regain altitude unsuccessfully. Steve remembered that he blessed himself and said, "God, make it quick or bring me through."

Using Steve's exact words …
"And then we hit. Now – the first time I tried to stand up – the black smoke hit me in the face and I went down. I tried once more.

Finally, I said to myself, 'You jerk. Hold your breath for a second like you were swimming.' And I got up. And there was a fella from Michigan and I had to push him out the window." Steve was able to escape through the window opening, too.

The crash pictures showed that the plane's twin tail sections were separated as the aircraft was cut in half. Steve suffered first degree burns on the right side of his face but miraculously he recovered the vision in his right eye. He suffered multiple cuts on his body as well. Of the 10 men on board the aircraft, 5 were killed and 5 survived.

Several months later when Steve was recovered enough to be sent back to the United States, he came out of the airplane and knelt down and kissed the ground. Later that day he learned that someone had stolen all of his clothes.

Steve, you are an amazing guy. Thank you for your bravery.

Al Bacchetta served in the Army, joining in 1943 when he was 19. He was assigned to a medical outfit that was sent to France and then marched into Germany. He arrived in the Dachau concentration camp as a liberator in 1945 – just as the War in Europe had ended. "It was really, really terrible," said Al. "I can still see it in my mind today. We saw things that we couldn't believe." We asked him how he found the courage to keep going after seeing so much tragedy and death and he replied, "We had to do whatever we could do for the people who survived the living hell of Dachau."Thank you, Al. Your contribution was amazing.

Tony Scozzafava was in the Navy in the early 1960s when he was assigned to the aircraft carrier USS Hancock CVA19. Tony remembered, "We went to Pearl Harbor and, going past the Arizona Memorial, we lined up on the deck in full dress uniform – and just the feeling. I could feel the hair on the back of my neck – it was so quiet."

PATRIOTISM

Here is a song we sang in Brooklyn where I grew up in the 1940s:

AMERICA, I LOVE YOU

America, I love you!
You're like a sweetheart of mine!
From ocean to ocean,
For you my devotion,
Is touching each boundary line.

Just like a little baby
Climbing it's mother's knee,
America, I love you!
And there's a hundred million others like me!

It was a very patriotic time in America after the Japanese attacked Pearl Harbor in December 1941 and the Germans declared war on us. We listened avidly to the news on the radio and read the newspaper daily (some newspapers had an evening edition as well). Since it was a time before television, we watched the newsreels on the giant movie screens and it was terrifying to watch the bombing of England and seeing our soldiers in battle. More than 400,000 American soldiers died during WWII. They were our true heroes.

Everyone in America took the War very seriously and we understood the sacrifices the soldiers were making to keep us free. Military people were greatly honored by our generation and deservedly so. We didn't ask for WWII but we certainly were not going to lose it.

The automobile industry came to a halt and the auto factories were turned into constructing aircraft. Getting new rubber tires for a car was next to impossible during WWII and the lessons learned during the Depression continued -- "Nothing should be wasted."

For those who stayed at home, our part of the War effort included doing without many necessities. The miracle drug penicillin was in short supply since it was needed for the soldiers on the front line.

Many young families couldn't afford to live independently while husbands went to war. Mothers and their small children often moved back home to live with their parents.

A person was given a ration card that indicated how much gasoline he was allowed to purchase depending on his need to drive a car for a war-related job, etc. Since gasoline was rationed, people didn't go on vacations very often. Trains were used to move troops so even taking a train ride wasn't easy to do.

Rationing was placed on sugar, flour, butter, milk, cheese, eggs, coffee, canned goods – even silk stockings.

An average family's income in 1940 was approximately $2,000 a year. Yet everyone was so patriotic they invested in War bonds to help fund the war. Bond stamps were sold for as little as 10 cents, and when the War bond stamp book was filled, the bond would be issued.

World War II War Bonds poster

Because meat was rationed, many people in Boonton began to raise chickens and even rabbits in their back yards. People were encouraged by the government to plant a "Victory Garden" to provide for their family's need for fruits and vegetables. This was a tremendous help to the government and one Internet site said that in 1946, when people suddenly stopped planting their victory gardens, there was a shortage of fruits and vegetables that year.

At the Royal Scarlet Grocery that Lloyd's parents owned they put pictures of soldiers in the window. "We called it the XYZ SOCIETY," Alice Charlton Heaton said. "We had a big bulletin board and the guys would write to my mom at the store and the letters were posted on the bulletin board so everybody could read them."

Margot Durrer was a teenager during the War and worried, "I remember knitting impossible scarves and socks – probably the poor soldiers couldn't even wear them."

Alice also recalls riding on a bus with other Boonton teenage girls who went to Fort Dix NJ to dance with the newly enlisted soldiers.

Bill Tredway remembered that during WWII, "Where the Town Hall now stands – that was a big tennis court and everybody in town contributed old pots and pans to be collected there since metal was needed for the War effort."

Tony Scozzafava told me, "I was a small child but I do remember blackouts, putting down the shades and a man on the street, Mr. George DeVera, who wore a metal helmet and had a big stick and a flashlight to make sure your lights were off, your shades were down and everyone was quiet. I remember they had round headlights on the cars and the top half of the headlights were painted black so the light would not be reflected up. The Air Raid siren would go off and it was scary. We were quiet and I waited to see Mr. DeVera going up and down the street."

Tony recalls, "I remember when I was a student in the Catholic school, Mt. Carmel, they thought a bomb would drop so we had to practice to get under the desk and put our heads down."

Lloyd's cousin Robert Charlton served during the War as a mechanic in the Air Force working on A20s and B26s. When asked if he ever worried about the War, he said matter-of-factly:

"We knew we would win WWII or die trying!"

When we asked Bill Bednar (who was stationed on Guam) what did he think about whether the United States would win, he said with incredulity:

"What did the Japanese expect? Did they actually think Americans would let the Germans and Japanese take over America?"

Bob Bogue, who served in a hospital unit in England during WWII, said the same thing when we asked if he thought America might lose the War:

"Never! We were invincible."

Paul Werner remembers marching up and down Main Street all night in celebration when the Japanese surrendered.

Betty Bandura remembers everybody was kissing everybody.

Joe Strelec recalls, "I remember when WWII was over and the horns were whistling and the people were going nuts on Main Street."

Lloyd had just come up out of the subway station in New York City's Times Square when VJ-Day was announced over a car radio parked nearby and in seconds Times Square looked like it does on New Year's Eve.

OUR PARENTS

Many of us had grandparents who came to America in the early 1900s. Steve Bolcar explained, "They came to find a better life." They were willing to do whatever it took to succeed and what they achieved in just one generation is awesome.

Our parents were strong and courageous. They would often walk several miles to get to work (or to church) and they put cardboard in their shoes to make them last longer. In a time before modern medicine, they experienced many hardships and yet they rarely cried. Their self-control was like iron and their 'will to survive' was indomitable. We grew up admiring our parents and appreciating all the sacrifices we saw them make for us. It was not uncommon for our parents to work a 6-day week and even on Sunday for one-half day. When they got their one week vacation every year -- it was often *without pay*.

Our parents had unwavering moral character and integrity. They worked hard, helped their neighbors and brought us up to respect our elders. We were reminded that nothing was OWED to us – but that, with hard work, we could succeed just as they had done. We were taught the value of honesty, kindness and patriotism. We were brought up to do hard work without complaining.

Many mothers sewed clothing for their children. Several people we interviewed remembered wearing pajamas made from bleached fabric that was originally used to pack chicken feed. Few store-bought Halloween costumes were used.

Our mothers spent all day on Monday – washday - using a wash board or a washing machine that had a wringer on top that pressed the water out of the clothes. Then - winter or summer – clothes were put on the line to dry. In the winter the towels would come back inside the house as stiff as a board and actually you could stand them up they were so frozen.

The miracle drug, penicillin, was not available until late in 1936. Therefore, most people we interviewed suffered a terrible family tragedy during their own childhood through an accident, illness or death of a family member.

Most women giving birth in the 1920s and early 1930s did not go to the hospital. Instead, children were delivered at home with the help of a midwife and the town doctor. Several people we interviewed suffered the heartbreaking loss of their mother in childbirth. The Internet (Wikipedia) stated these facts: The death rate from childbirth in 1900 was 1 woman in 100 around 1900

Our parents came from a 'melting pot generation.' Their next door neighbors might have emigrated from faraway places like Italy, Czechoslovakia, Finland, England, Germany, Austria, Scotland, Switzerland or Ireland. It was common for people of the same cultural background to live in the same neighborhoods, so the Flats area that was around Wilson and Kanouse Streets in Boonton was nicknamed "German town." The Hill was nicknamed "Cabbage Hill" because lots of Irish people settled there.

Down on Monroe Street where Al Bacchetta lived – (then Monroe Street was called Morris Avenue) he said:

"Next door was my aunt.
My grandparents lived across the street.
Two other aunts lived nearby.

It was like 'Little Italy.' And we all had big families:
I was 1 of 8 children,
My aunt next door had 9 or 10 kids, and
On the other side next door there were 6 or 7 kids.
Families were big. It was a time when neighbors helped each other."

JOBS AVAILABLE TO OUR PARENTS

Most people held jobs that were close to home. Their jobs included being: a piece-worker at the pocketbook factory, waiter, waitress, taxi driver, bartender, machine knitter, seamstress, manual laborer, secretary, gas station attendant, plumber, carpenter, baker, car salesman, employee at Van Raalte, Aircraft Radio or E.F. Drew, tool maker at Branson, mechanic and maintenance man.

They worked as delivery men bringing blocks of ice to homes, to town stores and, Charlie Marshall remembers, "We iced the refrigerated cars for E.F. Drew." There were chefs, roofers, bank managers and tellers, milk men, mail men, truck drivers, policemen and our oldest interview participant at 106 years old, Ann Barnish

Osterhoudt, packaged margarine at The Wacoline (later called E.F. Drew). There were auctioneers, domestics, Christmas tree salesmen, landscapers, JCP&L meter readers and farmers.

Betty Bandura said that her dad started as a railroad porter and rose to be freight and track manager, and was offered a Vice Presidency. Some parents held prestigious jobs such as attorneys, foremen and controllers. Swiss-born Othmar Ammann came to America as a young man and settled in Boonton. He was a civil engineer and he is famous for designing many important bridges, including the George Washington Bridge.

Al Condon told us his mother worked at the "Sewing Room" on Main and Liberty, a door or two up from where the old A&P used to be.

Lloyd's dad, Frank Charlton, had a wife and three small children to support and during the Great Depression he could not find work as a carpenter. He went to a friend and offered to build a building on the friend's vacant lot (most recently that building was known as *The Castaway Shop*) and in exchange he would become the first tenant. He opened a store called The Royal Scarlet Grocery. When Lloyd's dad expanded his business he took space in the Brady Building which is where Lloyd and Al Condon met. Al lived in an upstairs apartment over the store. After WWII that building was sold and torn down to make room for a used car lot.

In the early part of the century, careers open to women were limited to secretary, nurse and teacher.

Part time jobs:

Shoveled snow
Delivered newspaper for Mr. Basch on Birch & Mechanic Streets at 6 a.m.
Worked in the family business
     i.e., grocery, trucking company
Babysat
Delivered telegrams
(FYI: Sending a telegram was how you contacted someone during an emergency. A telegram was sent if a soldier was injured or died during the War.)
Usher at the State Theater
Employed at Frankels clothing
Employed in card company on Cornelia Street
Employed at Alfie's store
Counselor at Camp Morris
Dishwasher
Picked string beans for .01 per lb.

Picked strawberries in Montville
Employed at Segals Shoe Store dusting shoes and stocking shelves
Soda jerk at Cornelia Pharmacy
Sold magazines like:
       The Saturday Evening Post
       Liberty
       Radio Mirror
       Movie Mirror and
       Physical Culture

Most of us took part-time jobs during high school. Hands down – the best job was held by Bill Nikel. During WWII, finding men to fill jobs was hard to do so the Fuller Brush company hired Bill as a "Fuller Brush Boy."

"I loved it!" said Bill. "I had a big basket on my bicycle and I would put the sample case in it and knock on a door and I would say, *'Well, Madam, I have this gift for you. Here's a lapel brush.'* And another gift was a little red plastic comb. This is what you call 'door-openers.' A fiber broom was $1.19 and the big ones were $1.69. Trying to deliver the large brooms and mops, I had to ride one-handed on my bike and hold the broom out in my other hand."

JOBS AVAILABLE IN OUR GENERATION

We made our parents proud. Here are some careers held by the people we interviewed: Medical doctor, test engineer for Picatinny, advertising agency owner, police sergeant, two police chiefs, owner of a trucking business, Wall Street financier, foreman, district manager, marketing specialist, VP in insurance, department store buyer, Naval Intelligence officer, baker, executive at Norda, carpenter, radio/TV engineer, college professor and executive accountant.

In that era, many women stayed at home with their preschool children. When the kids reached high school age the women took jobs nearby, for example, at the local bank, Newberry's 5 & 10 department store, waitress, legal secretary in town or at the Morristown Courthouse, piece worker at the pocketbook factory, office assistant and receptionist at Bell Labs.

Lloyd's sister Alice Heaton graduated in 1943 and was recruited by Bell Labs to be trained as a draftsman. Since the young men graduating high school were immediately drafted into the military, Bell Labs was willing to train women for jobs that usually were given to men. Women proved to be capable in a wide range of careers that were formerly opened only to men.

VOLUNTEERS

Just about everyone we interviewed talked about their volunteer activities in Boonton:

Little League coach etc.
Hospital receptionist
Running a second-hand store at the Castaway
Running the thrift shop
Fireman
Kiwanis Ambulance volunteer
Women's Auxiliary of Fire Dept.
Working the concessions stands at the yearly 3-day Firemen's Carnival
Scout leader
Alderman
Board of Education
Other political office
Bounce (Boonton United Community Effort)
Sunday school teacher
Choir member
Historical Society members

NAME CHANGES WE HEARD ABOUT IN OUR INTERVIEWS:

Gaylord's Gate was sold to Scerbo Pontiac
Scerbo Pontiac is now the Boonton Avenue Grill
West Main Street was originally Schultz Street; the last block of West Main Street became Hawkins Place
Boonton Avenue was Brook Street
Lorraine Terrace was the site of Hillary's Pond, later called Sunset Lake
Wilson School was called St. John's
Harrison Street School became a synagogue and is now a Mosque
Pilgrim Apartments was originally called the Darress Arms
Monroe Street was once Morris Avenue
Our Lady of Mt. Carmel Roman Catholic Church was originally named St. Mary's

BUSES AROUND TOWN WERE:

Bus #116 went to Newark.
Bus #80 was a route to Paterson.
Bob Klindt ran a bus that went to Morristown.

EVENTS AROUND TOWN: LABOR DAY PARADE

The firemen's parade on Labor Day is held on the Saturday of Labor Day weekend and it is followed by a carnival that went on all weekend. I've enclosed some photos from the Carnival so you can see how spectacular it is for a small town. Lloyd's cousin Robert said that when he was a kid he would go down when they were setting up the rides (originally the carnival was held at the West Boonton Ball Field behind what is now King's Supermarket) and they would let him have free rides on the merry-go-round, ferris wheel and the swings while they made their adjustments.

The Labor Day Firemen's Parade participants had to march uphill. Later the location for the end of the parade was changed to the Boonton High School field so marchers then marched 'downhill' on Main Street toward the school.

Cousin Robert Charlton said he used to go down to the Fair after it closed and check around the various booths looking for coins that people dropped. "I used to make a couple of dollars that way," he said.

Tony Scozzafava remembered "A friend bought a raffle ticket at the Elks Club and gave it to my father and my father won a banjo clock. I still have it."

Tony Scozzafava loved marching with the American Legion Band and wearing an outfit that was similar to the West Point cadet's uniform with the black plume on the head gear and a gray uniform.

Boonton's Harmony Drum Corps is very much a part of Boonton's celebrations and the drum corps came into existence in 1886. Bill Bednar remembers they performed at Yankee Stadium between games of a double header several times.

MEMORIAL DAY CEREMONY

Boonton honors Memorial Day each year when the town folk come together to pay tribute to the men and women who served in the military.

The Boy Scouts go to each town cemetery and place a flag on the grave of anyone who served in the military. Folk artist, Ann Reeves, who went to Boonton High School and lived in Boonton when she got married, has painted her tribute to Boonton's Memorial Day.

As part of the ceremony, the name of each Boonton person who died during War is read. Wreaths are presented by various civic groups as well as the churches in town and placed at the War monument at City Hall. Then three men who fought during WWII fire their rifles three times in memory of the brave soldiers who died for us so we could live free.

ILLNESSES AND ACCIDENTS

"A typical household experienced the usual diseases we see today – asthma, appendicitis, tonsillitis, bronchitis, chicken pox, mumps, measles, German measles, whooping cough, pleurisy and ear infection. However, hanging a 'quarantine' sign over a door in the 1920s and 1930s indicated that the family might have received a diagnosis of polio, scarlet fever, rheumatic fever, diphtheria and the dreaded disease called 'consumption' which was also called tuberculosis.

Common cures used by families in a time before penicillin included taking cod liver oil, using mustard plaster, camphor oil, mutton tallow (fat from lamb rendered and rubbed on the chest), garlic was worn by a string around your neck and/or you would eat garlic. A bracelet of onions was thought to bring down a fever. People used horse liniment, a spoonful of kerosene with sugar, milk of magnesia and the most unique cure was rendering skunk grease and rubbing it on your chest.

Mary Carmen told this story, "One day my mother took me out of the crib and put me down on the floor. I think I was about 4-1/2 and then I wouldn't stand up. I kept falling down. And she thought I was playing with her. She said, 'Come on now, I've got a lot to do today.' Then I started crying," said Mary. "So then my mother knew something was wrong." It was polio and Mary did recover but she was left with a residual limp and a weak leg.

With so many overwhelming difficulties to endure, there were a few parents who had nervous breakdowns. One cure used during the 1940s was a lobotomy and another was shock treatments.

We can laugh when Gladys Franchi says she got her tongue stuck frozen to the school swing, but we have to cry when Steve Bolcar describes how he was born in 1917 and both he and his mother were diagnosed with the '1918 flu epidemic.' Years later, a friend told Steve she was at All Soul's Hospital in Morristown and remembered hearing Steve's mother begging to be allowed to see her newborn son. Tragically, she died. Amazingly, baby Steven, then age 1 year, survived this epidemic.

Lucille Hopkins Scerbo said, "When I was 12 years old I had St. Vitus's Dance. It developed after having rheumatic fever." The Internet said St. Vitus's dance is characterized by involuntary muscular movements of the face and extremities as a result of an acute disturbance of the central nervous system. There is no specific treatment.

Lucille recalls, "My father used to hold me down to keep me from jumping all over the place when I first got it. And they gave me a baby bottle for nourishment because I couldn't hold anything. They didn't expect me to live through my teens," Lucille said. The family worried that her heart muscle would be affected and miraculously that did not happen.

Don Estler was a child of 5 when his father was diagnosed with encephalitis (sleeping sickness). Encephalitis is an acute inflammation of the brain. Before his father's illness, Don remembers the family hired both a maid and chauffeur and lived in their own home. As Don remembers, "My dad was an officer of a bank called The Brooklyn Savings Bank. When I was 5 years of age he came down with encephalitis supposedly because of a tsetse fly, but it was probably a tick as I don't know any tsetse flies around Boonton. He lost his job. In those days, even though he was an officer in a bank, he only got a 5-year medical retirement pension plan."

Just a few years later, Don's older brother Whitfield Estler died at the age of 14 from complications resulting from an undiagnosed mastoid infection. In a time before modern medicine, it was not unusual for people to die of diseases that could easily be cured today with the use of penicillin. Whitfield died in June 1936 and penicillin came into use in September 1936. Lloyd remembers when he was 8 or 9 years old his mother, Virginia, sent him across the street to Don's house to ask about Whitfield and he had to go home and tell her Whitfield died.

"The teacher picked me to be a polar bear" said 8 year old Betty Bandura excitedly to her mother when she returned from school. "I am to wear my white Communion dress and white veil to school tomorrow and the six of us will walk down the aisle in church." Betty was not a polar bear. In fact Betty was chosen to walk down the aisle in church accompanying the little white casket of her classmate who had suddenly died. Betty has been chosen to be a 'pallbearer.'

Betty Bandura also remembers as a young girl, "My sister Florence was in her first year of high school and was tested for tuberculosis. Dad called in five doctors but they couldn't do anything. She was in the hospital but wanted to die at home. She was 16 when she died. They burned all our clothes and cleaned the house thoroughly as it was a contagious disease. I never got over it and even today I cry when I remember her."

When there was a death in the family a black wreath was put on the front door and the deceased person's body was laid out in the living room at home for several days. This was in a time before air conditioning. Mourners were expected to wear black not only during the wake and burial, but for an entire year after the loved one's death.

Dixie Croce Perry was a young girl when her 19 year old brother Willie Croce accidentally drowned in the swimming area of Grace Lord Park called "Deep Hole." It was a very sad time and Dixie said, "I still cry when I think about it."

Margot Ammann Durrer was not quite a teenager when she faced tragedy. "My mother died of breast cancer when I was 11."

Julia Dunn recalled, "I was 7 years old and it was very sad when my brother, who was one month old, died."

Gloria McCormick told us, "When I was about 3 years old, my mother was diagnosed with tuberculosis. In those days tuberculosis was prevalent and there were no cures. The sick person was usually sent to a sanitarium to breathe fresh cold air." In her case, Gloria and her sister had to stay with extended family for three years because the disease was very contagious. She returned home only after her mother's death when she was 6 years old.

Gilda Adams was in the 8th grade when her mother died. "In those days the wake was in the house – like for 3 days – and when I go into a florist today the smell of roses reminds me again of that awful time."

Marie DiEduardo at the age of 5 lost her mother who died in childbirth. She also lost two siblings when she was a young child. When she grew up and got married to Nano DiEduardo they moved to Boonton. She was the mother of four preschool children when her husband Nano tragically died in a farming accident. "There was no such thing as insurance back in those days. I went to work at Boonton Handbag and Mr. Patasnik was the owner. You couldn't find a nicer person than him." "Marie," we said in shock, "Where did you find the courage to go on?" Marie replied simply and quietly, "You got through it because you have no choice. Also I put my trust in God and He helped."

Sadly, Marie suffered the worst punishment a parent can endure when her oldest son Joseph died of complications of a wound he received while serving in Vietnam. His 18 military service medals, including the Medal of Honor, are displayed proudly on a bookcase in her living room. It was only when she talked about her son that Marie had to fight back her tears.

After Marie had successfully raised four children and she retired from work, she did something remarkable. Marie took vacations to Peru, Argentina, Brazil, Chile, Kenya, most of the countries of Europe, India, China, Japan, Egypt, Australia, New Zealand, Hawaii and Alaska – to name just the trips I recall that she mentioned! Marie's indomitable spirit has much to teach us about true courage and not letting adversity dominate your life.

VENDORS IN BOONTON

This was the part of our interview that I loved hearing about -- the vendors who came through Boonton:

- There was a vendor who sold coffee.
- The insurance man was Roy Bockman. George Hezlitt remembers, "It was 4 cents for us to be insured and he would drive to our house to pick up the money."
- Mr. Baginsky collected trash.
- Mr. Leone collected scrap iron. Fred Ludwig remembers that Mr. Leone had his junk yard on Old Boonton Road and that his truck had old cow bells on it that he rang when he rode through the neighborhood.
- Charlie Marshall remembers, "My father had a milk business, as well as an ice and wood business for quite a number of years." Charlie said, "Frank Estler was in the ice business during the early 1900s. My dad cut ice from Estler's pond.   Dixon sold my father their ice business and we had the

business until 1968. Our biggest customer was Drew Chemical. We used to ice their refrigerated cars."

- Lloyd remembers his cousin Bud Charlton delivering ice used for Lloyd's family's ice box (in a time before refrigerators).
- In a time when most homes were heated with coal furnaces, Lloyd's Uncle Harry Charlton had a coal delivery business.
- Harry Charlton also went into the oil business back then and eventually sold his business to Dixon Oil.

-

- A Dugan's Bakery truck rode through town every day. If you put a Dugan's sign in your front window, the salesman knew to stop by.
- A milk man delivered bottles of milk to the back door of the house at 5 a.m. each day. Milk was not homogenized. Sometimes in the winter the bottles would freeze and the frozen milk pushed up the cap on the bottle an inch or two. Since milk was not homogenized, the part that would be pushed to the top was cream and it tasted wonderful.
- Julia Dunn remembered that someone came in a truck from Paterson and sold fruits and vegetables.
- Betty Bandura was a little girl and she vaguely recalls a person named "Cobb" who would sell live chickens and then ring their necks after you purchased them. Betty recalls, "I was a little girl and I would say emphatically to my mother – 'There will be no chickens for our house!!'"
- Bob Bogue remembered a man selling brooms called a Fuller Brush man.
- There was an Italian guy from Newark who sold fish. Steve Bolcar said, "He had a big basket and he carried the fish on his shoulder."
- Mr. Jacobus came from Montville with fruits and vegetables. Steve Bolcar believed they charged five cents for an apple.
- Gladys Franchi remembers a vendor who would call out "Hey – watermelon – 5 cents!"
- Mr. Garafolo sold fresh produce and he also sold Christmas trees from his truck.

- Mary Carmen remembers someone named Mr. Young who sold vegetables in her neighborhood.
- Mae Wiswall remembers on Boonton Avenue that there was a hurdy gurdy vendor who had a monkey who danced when the man turned the music grinder machine.
- Edna Austin remembers a tailor who came to her house to show her father new suiting fabric.
- Tony Scozzafava remembers a laundry man delivering freshly starched shirts to his house.
- Betty Bandura remembers the McCormick bakery truck coming every Saturday.
- Ernestine Cascella remembers an Italian grocer from Paterson who brought different kinds of cheeses and tomatoes used in Italian cooking.
- Gloria McCormick remembers when houses were heated by coal she loved to watch the truck put a chute into a basement window and send the coal down the chute. It was always dirty and dusty.
- Bill Nikel remembers Manfredonia Bakery delivering bread and cakes to his house.
- Ann Barnish Osterhoudt, the oldest person we have interviewed (currently she is 106!), told us that Hobart Marshall delivered ice to her house using a horse and wagon.
- Harry Reeves remembers a vendor who sold eggs.
- Al Bacchetta said someone named Abe Summers sold watermelon and vegetables.
- Jim McGlone remembers a man with an old bus who sold canned goods and cereals from his bus.
- Betty Bandura remembers that the Hollacks (phonetic) came to her house to sell tea and soap.
- Ruth Halstead is sure the butcher came to their house because she remembers he would always give Ruth a piece of baloney when he came.
- Dixie Perry recalls fondly, "We had everything!! Chickens – watermelons – and we'd all run out to the 'running board' of the truck to get a piece of ice. We had a man who came with a parrot. The parrot would pick up a paper from a box and give it to you and it told your fortune!"

GROWING UP IN BOONTON

There were lots of friends who lived nearby. Also, there were always lots of cousins who lived nearby.

Older kids were allowed to go out to play early in the morning and they did not have to go home until dinner time.

Children did not have a lot of clothing. Gilda remembers she got two new outfits for school every year. Also, clothing was purchased two sizes too big so kids could grow into it – which would take a year or two.

Girls wore dresses to school until the late 1960s. Boys wore short pants (even in winter) until the 4th grade and then three-quarter length pants, called knickers, until the 8th grade. Here's a photo of Lloyd wearing knickers and his younger brother Jack wearing shorts.

Long corduroy pants were worn by boys in high school and dungarees were not permitted to be worn to school until the late 1960s.

Lee Geier said, "During the Depression we had a telephone, but kids were not allowed to use the phone because it was too expensive. So I built my own telephone to talk to Doris Crane, next door. I used two tin cans and a kite string and that did the job. You had to keep tension on the string or it wouldn't work."

Joe Strelec told us, "I remember in our house there was a big potbelly stove in the living room and everybody fought for a position behind it – as we got dressed for school near the heat." One of Joe's fondest memories was getting three sets of underwear as a gift because he knew it had been a big sacrifice to buy new underwear for him.

Saturday night was bath night. Lloyd's mother would heat water in a large tea kettle on the kitchen stove and carry it upstairs to the bathtub because much of the time they did not have hot water in the faucets. It was not uncommon for the children to share the same bath water. Several people we interviewed did not have indoor plumbing when they were small children in the 1930s.

Cereal boxes offered coupons. If you collected enough coupons and mailed them in, you might get a Code Ring! Lloyd remembered that he collected enough cereal box tops to get a ticket to the rodeo in Madison Square Garden.

Danny Bonanni and Betty Bandura each admitted to sneaking into the Lyceum Theater even though it was officially closed and was being used as a storage place.

Edna Austin said as a small child she used to cross the street by crawling through the storm sewer on William Street.

Fred and Paul Ludwig would get up early and go to the Tourne Park in the winter at 6 a.m. so they could ski before they went to school.

Kids looked for soda bottles to return to the grocery for the 2-cent deposit money. That was a quick and easy way to earn enough money to go to the movies.

"One of my happiest memories was spending Saturday afternoon at The State Theater," said just about everyone we interviewed. "You walked in under the screen and the audience was facing you."

Kids would go to the Tourne Park (which was not a public park but was owned privately by Mr. DeCamp. There were paths in the Tourne maintained by Mr. DeCamp.

Fred Ludwig said, "We built cabins in the Tourne when Mr. DeCamp owned it. We brought axes and we built beautiful cabins and we slept there."

Mr. DeCamp lived on West Main Street near Lake Avenue. Lloyd remembered Mr. DeCamp had a tree about a foot in diameter growing right in the middle of his house and up through the roof.

An afternoon at Grace Lord Park, Indian Steps or the Water Tower on Sheep Hill always guaranteed fun.

Sometimes when young people went roller skating they used their own shoe skates, but Grace Condon remembered having clamp-on roller skates that fit over a regular shoe. She would share her skates with a friend and they would pump with one foot and wear a skate on the other foot.

Ruth Halstead and Fran Gibian remember that they went together to a big roller skating rink in Florham Park and that is where Fran met her husband. Fran remembers that her parents told her they used to ice skate back and forth on the Morris Canal from Boonton to Dover!

Gilda remembers coloring books about the Dionne quintuplets – Emilie, Marie, Yvonne, Annette, Cecile who were born in 1934.

When Gilda was a little girl she was so in love with Hopalong Cassidy she wrote a letter to Bill Boyd and received a signed photograph!

For many families, the Sunday ritual included going to church in the morning and then stopping at a local bakery to buy some delicious buns and rolls. Mother would cook a big dinner which was often served in the early afternoon. It might be a pot roast, meatloaf, chicken, leg of lamb, ham or, if the family was Italian, they served things like sausage, meatballs, lasagna, ravioli and spaghetti. Meals would have to be stretched if company dropped by. The rule was called "FHB" which meant 'family hold back' and everyone knew they were to take smaller portions so there would be enough food for the guests.

Dinner was served on Sunday at the dining room table and Al Bacchetta said, "I remember the old timers would sit for hours and hours and talk after dinner. Not today. Today when people finish eating they run to the TV to watch the ball game."

Birthday parties long ago were not the lavish parties that are seen today. A typical birthday party would consist of serving a cake or cupcakes and perhaps getting a pair of gloves as a gift. Being photographed was a rare thing to do. Edna Austin remembers the thrill of having her picture taken every year on her birthday. One person we interviewed never had a picture taken of her until the school graduation photo!

If a family had a piano they were very lucky. People we interviewed recalled fondly that a parent or sibling could play piano or that they were allowed to take piano lessons themselves.

People used an ice box before refrigerators came into use. It cost 10 cents for a large chunk of ice which was delivered by the iceman every few days.

Some kids remember that their dads made their own wine in the basement and there was a fruit vendor who kept a supply of ingredients used to make liqueurs hidden on his truck for those who 'knew' to ask for them.

It was rumored that some vendors or store keepers took 'numbers bets.'

Everyone remembered during war time when they purchased white margarine with a yellow button in the middle that you had to burst so it would make the margarine turn yellow to look like actual butter.

When WWII ended, young people began getting married on a shoestring, often returning to their parents' home to live after a small ceremony performed in the church rectory or by a Justice of the Peace. Having a wedding reception at home was common, and Doris Hornick remembered buying new 'paper' curtains to decorate the house for her wedding.

Honeymoons usually were planned for only a few days, and the destinations were nearby – New York City, Niagara Falls, Atlantic City, Pennsylvania, Washington DC or Virginia Beach. Lloyd's cousin Robert was in the military at the time he got married, so he considered their trip back to the Army base in Texas as their honeymoon.

Marriage, for better or worse, was considered a vow and no senior citizen we interviewed has gotten divorced.

Lucille Scerbo remembers receiving a board game that was called "The 1939 World's Fair Game." It was similar to Monopoly but the buildings were called the Trylon and Perisphere.

Parents were strict and not very demonstrative. A common theme went like this: "Can I please go, daddy?" Then father would reply, "What did your mother say?" And when the child admitted that mom said "NO" then father would echo, "Then it is no."

Words like 'please' and 'thank you' were used by everyone. We were taught to respect the elderly and often a grandparent would live with the family.

Coal was used to heat most homes so children had chores including putting out the ashes, taking out the garbage, washing the supper dishes, dusting and cleaning, babysitting a younger sibling, doing the laundry and helping with ironing. It was part of the daily routines of family life and everyone was required to help around the house.

Table manners and Emily Post's etiquette book were part of our traditions, too. Did you know that it was rude to pick up a fork at the dinner table before mother sat down and picked up her fork?

Adults believed there was 'honor in work' and would take any job rather than to accept handouts or ask for welfare assistance.

Parents had expectations and children lived up to them. We were taught to be respectful. If a child went beyond the boundaries of house rules, he could expect a swift spanking. And if a neighbor or school teacher called your mother to complain about your behavior, you were sure to get into trouble at home!

It was common for young people to hitchhike to the next town, and many adults did that, too. There was little traffic and very few families owned a car.

It was not uncommon for a family to take in a 'boarder' as a source of income.

Kids did not have wrist watches or cell phones long ago. It was common to hear a parent call out of a window, "Come home, Terry, it is time for dinner."

Everyone was struggling financially and there was no shame attached to it. However, since most families had two parents, children in one-family homes felt a stigma about that. Divorce was never mentioned. There was a "don't ask' and 'don't tell' mentality. Children didn't even feel comfortable asking their own parent about the missing parent.

Having a telephone in Boonton was common although many people had a party line. If your telephone had a 'letter' in the identification, for- example "83W" - that meant you had a party line and you didn't answer the phone until it rang a certain number of times.

Most families had a dog or a cat for a pet, but once in a while we interviewed a person who had a bird, a possum or a goat for a pet.

With such large families, it was not uncommon to have two double beds in one bedroom to sleep four children.

Homes did not have air conditioning until the 1950s.

Grace Condon remembers the kids played jump rope during school recess and she was pretty good at jumping. We played jump rope all the time in Brooklyn where I grew up and I remember some of the chants we would sing as we gestured while jumping rope:

"The Clock Stands Still While the Hands Turns Around." Then one girl was designated as the 'hand on the clock' and she had to jump in a circle around the other girl who was designed as the 'clock.

Some card games were Pinochle, Hearts, Canasta, Bridge, Rummy, War, Knuckles, Solitaire and Old Maid.

Hopscotch and pickup-sticks were fun, too, as well as
Tag
Hide and Seek
Giant Steps
Red Light, Green Light
Leap Frog
Kick the Can and
Ringalevio

Paper dolls and coloring books were a necessity for long hot summer afternoons and it was a very big treat to get a big box of Crayola crayons.

Jigsaw puzzles were often worked on at the dining room table and the family would gather round together. This was a time when the young folks would ask family questions and the older family members would tell stories of how they came to America, or where they got married, how many brothers and sisters they had, etc.

A high-bouncing ball could keep us occupied for hours. One game played by Grace Condon was called *"Russia"* and Grace said you had to throw the ball against a wall, then you had to spin in a circle (or perform some other feat) before catching the ball.

I remember we played hand-clapping games together and we still see young girls today doing the same thing. I remember playing with a pink Spalding bouncing ball and chanting rhymes in alphabetical order like this:

"A my name is Alice and my husband's name is Al.
We come from America and we sell Apples.
B my name is Barbara and my husband's name is Bill.
We come from Bermuda ... "

Boys played marbles, bottle cap games, collected and traded baseball cards (the cards came in a package with a piece of gum that tasted like powdered shoe leather) and most of all – they played pick-up games of softball, baseball, football or basketball depending on the season.

Lloyd recalled that he once got a few friends together and they challenged Paul Ludwig and his friends from the "Riverside Athletic Club" to a pickup game of baseball. In nine innings Paul struck out 23 of them.

Very few kids had an official baseball bat or catcher's mitt. Any wooden stick would do! Fred Ludwig said that once in a while when he was watching a baseball game, a foul ball would come his way and he might stomp the ball into the ground to hide it. Then when the game was over he would go back and retrieve the ball. Fred also said, if a bat was broken and discarded, he would take it home and tape the broken bat with black tape and it worked just fine.

When we interviewed Ann (Barnish) Osterhoudt (she is currently 106 years old), she described a game she played called either 'piggy' or 'peggy.' You carved a stick to a point and laid it on the ground. Then you stepped on the point to get it to fly up in the air and you would then take another stick and hit it as far as it would go. When we interviewed Steve Bolcar (who was a dozen years younger than Ann) he described playing the same game.

Board games like chess, checkers, backgammon and Monopoly were as popular back then as they are today.

Bike riding was a luxury and not many kids owned a bike. Everyone wanted to own a Schwinn, Raleigh 21 or Roll Fast. In Boonton you could rent a bike at the building that was most recently used as the "Castaways Shop."

In fact, Lloyd remembers you could rent a 'bicycle built for two' at that store! Terry remembers in Brooklyn they could rent a bicycle for $.35 for an hour.

Fred Ludwig remembers building a go-cart. He told me, "We used roller skates – a large box – and a couple of cans from cat food for headlights – and two pieces of wood for handles."

Scouting was popular and Danny Bonanni remembers, "You didn't have sleeping bags or all the equipment that is sold today." You just grabbed a blanket and went camping with friends often without adult leaders.

Scouting began in February 1910 and Boonton had a Troop by September 1910 so this is a tradition with a long history. Boonton's Troop 1 has been operating continuously for 100 years!!!! Lloyd has been involved in scouting for 60 years, and was a Scout Master for 15 years, as well as co-founding Cub Pack 201 with his first wife, Ann, as well as served on many committees too numerous to mention.

Halloween in Boonton included "mischief night" where the teenagers would ring a doorbell and run away. When town folk complained of ruined gardens, it was decided that Boonton would have a parade down Main Street to the Fire House on

Washington Street on Halloween night. There they would award prizes for the best costumes, and all the children who participated in the parade would be given candy by the Fire Department. That parade still exists today and probably dates back more than 60 years.

On Halloween kids enjoyed getting dressed in costumes. Unlike today, the costumes were homemade and generally kids would go into the attic for old-fashioned clothes, or they would dress like a hobo. Part of the fun of Halloween was that people had to guess who you actually were. Paul Werner said, "No matter what I did everyone knew who I was because I was always the tallest kid in the class."

Speaking of Halloween, Paul Werner said he joined the Civil Defense in his adolescence. The Internet says that the Civil Defense was a group "who performed nonmilitary activities designed to protect civilians and their property from enemy actions in time of war."

Anyway, Paul remembers, "I was riding with a special cop on Halloween and we stopped a bunch of kids and asked, 'What do you have in your pocket?' The cop deliberately tapped the boy's pocket and it was pocket filled with raw eggs."

CHRISTMAS

Tony Scozzafava remembers that you had to put tinsel on the Christmas tree and it was a very tedious job because you were supposed to hang one strand of tinsel at a time. (I remember that, too!)

For some families, a favorite Christmas memory was going to Midnight Mass on Christmas Eve and then coming home to a house filled with lots of family and lots of gifts under the tree.

Don Estler's memory was that Santa came on Christmas Eve after he and his brother Whitfield went to bed and Santa brought a Christmas tree for them which he then decorated complete with a miniature train and village under the tree. And there would be gifts galore!

Bobby Banks, Morris County's first Black Police Chief who served from 1990 to 1995, told this story about Christmas when he was 12 years old. "On Christmas morning I came downstairs and I am looking around – no bicycle. After the gifts were opened, my mother asks me to get her a cup of water and so I go in the kitchen and turn on the light – and there was the bike! Wow! I had the best mom in the world!" We couldn't help but notice that Bob's memory of that Christmas still brings a smile to his face.

The Elks Club gave a Christmas party where Santa would distribute candy and a gift to each poor child in Boonton. If parents didn't have money for lavish gifts they might knit a sweater or create a toy that was handmade. Since Lloyd's dad was a carpenter, he gave Lloyd's sister Alice a doll house and he gave Lloyd and his brother Jack a handmade miniature golf set that they loved to play with as children.

Bill Birch recalls among his most cherished childhood memories was when his father and mother made things for the kids at Christmas. "My dad made a wonderful dollhouse for my sister and each room had wallpaper and my mother probably did that. He made a barn for my brother and me and we could lift up one side of the barn and there were animals inside."

CHURCH MEMORIES

I remember that as a Catholic girl I always had to have my head covered when we entered a Catholic church. If a hat wasn't available, a girl was expected to put a Kleenex on her head. Catholic folks were not allowed to eat meat on Friday and the Church rule was that, in order to receive Holy Communion, a person had to refrain from eating any food after midnight on Saturday night. Altar boys were always boys. Girls were prohibited from serving at Mass or on the church altar.

If a Catholic young woman was invited to be in a wedding party of a non-Catholic friend, she had to refuse the invitation as it was forbidden for a Catholic to take part in ceremonies held in other churches.

SCHOOL

Regarding school memories, Lloyd's sister Alice remembers it was 4th or 5th grade when Coach Shriner gave them a card on which they would get a check mark when they were able to perform a somersault, a back somersault, a headstand, a pyramid, elephant walk, etc. "I was not able to do a headstand and I don't think I ever did a somersault either," said Alice.

Mr. Mann had students recite poems. Lee Geier remembers reciting WORK and TREES by Joyce Kilmer. He also recalled a John Masefield poem that began with the words, "I must go down to the seas again."

Don Estler remembers his favorite pen was a fountain pen with a little lever on the side of the pen that sucked up ink from an inkwell.

Lloyd remembers being in the Army in 1946and paying $8 in the military store (called a PX) to buy the latest invention, a ball point pen.

Ann Reeves remembered they had "dress-up Friday" at Boonton High School.

Don Estler told us his favorite part of high school was playing in the 'swing' band, being in the orchestra, the marching band and taking part in school plays.

Gladys Franchi remembers, "You had to be elected to the cheerleading squad" and it was very exciting when she won!

Harry Reeves was proud when he was chosen as a school crossing guard and he even thinks he wore a badge.

OTHER MEMORIES

Asked about her favorite toy, Ann Barnish Osterhoudt (born in 1904) said she didn't have many toys and that earning money was her favorite thing to do.

E.F. Drew used to dump waste at Jerry's field behind Green Street and eventually the government created a "superfund" to clean the space, which is now Pepe's field and playground.

Lloyd's dad had a grocery store called The Royal Scarlet. Alice remembers the checkout clerk (her) did not swipe food items through an electric machine to tally how much was being spent. Instead, since the cash register did not add up the purchases, the register clerk would list the information on a brown paper bag, ex:

5 cents +
5 cents +
15 cents +
10 cents = 35 cents.

Then the clerk would manually add up the long list of items at lightning speed, and ring up the total purchase at the cash register. By age 13 Lloyd's sister Alice was capable of running the store.

When Interstate Highway Route 287 was being constructed, the town lost a shoe store, an ice cream store, Mr. Caval's barber shop and a few others.

In the 1940s, cigarettes cost $.15 per pack for name brands and 12 cents for off brands.

The Boonton Molding Company invented plastic dishware. It was called Boontonware.

When Boonton celebrated its 100th anniversary in 1967 the men in town were encouraged to grow a beard and become "Brothers of the Brush" to mimic the style of the late 1800s when many men wore beards. Fred Ludwig still wears his beard.

Newberry's Department Store relocated its store from Main Street near Plane Street. Paul Werner remembers that when they dug the basement for the Newberry building on Main Street at Boonton Avenue, the basement kept filling with water. Newberry had to get sump pumps because this new building was located at a site that was originally called "Brook Street" because a brook ran down that road – now Boonton Avenue.

People dressed up to vote in town and went to the State Theater to wait to hear election results in the 1940s.

Margot Ammann Durrer remembers in the 1940s there was double daylight savings time. When she left for school at 7 a.m. it was still dark outside.

Sunset Lake was offered to the town for $25,000 but the town didn't want the property. The owner sold the land to developers who developed it as Lorraine Terrace.

There was a tennis court that had to be removed when City Hall was built.

Local banks offered a free toaster to get new customers.

The State Theater would hold "bank night" on Tuesday. People would go down to the theater and buy a movie ticket and then they were entered into the drawing which had a $100 prize. They would stand around at the hall on Cornelia Street, next to the dentist's house (Dr. Bider). It was called the Three Links Hall. Then over a loudspeaker the winning number was announced. Kids would stand around collecting the unused movie tickets and then the kids would go in into the movie theater to see the second showing for free.

Mr. Spurway taught math. He had lost both of his arms in an accident.

Ernestine Cascella remembers there was a "Fashion Club" in high school.

Friday in school was dress-up day and Ann Reeves loved to wear fun outfits; for instance, she remembers wearing a silver long dress with silver ballerina shoes.

Artist, Ann Reeves, lived in Parsippany but at that time Parsippany had no high school so the children all went to Boonton High School. She envied the kids who lived in Boonton because there were so many wonderful stores in town. She loved how everyone could meet together and walk to the local ice cream parlor. And "Oh, the houses!" she recalls. "To me they looked like mansions. There were porches with lights on them and I think that is where I got my love for painting houses. I fell in love with the town."

Robert Charlton lived on West Main Street and walked to the John Hill School. He recalled, "It didn't matter if it snowed or rained or hailed – we always went to school."

Ms. Pat Fowler, a kindergarten teacher for 50 years, knew your name even when she met you 50 years later. The year she became 100 and was Grand Marshall of the Santa Parade there was a party for her at the Elks Clubs and she recognized and called by name many of her students from many years ago.

Julia Dunn said her half-sister, Mother Joseph of the Dominican Order, founded Caldwell College around 1939.

Bill Birch remembers that his grandfather was interested in helping Boonton and to this day there is a "Ross Scholarship" given to a Boonton senior high school student. George Ross was the first head of the hospital built in Boonton. The Community Medical Group was started by George Ross and Lloyd remembers as a teenager he had his tonsils taken out there.

Margot Durrer remembers that her parents "Blessed me with an upbringing that taught me to have an obligation to society – to learn – to share – and to give back. Life was not just about having fun."

Gladys Franchi remembers that Mr. Boyd was instrumental in getting the first ambulance in Boonton. She and her sisters would walk up Main Street behind the ambulance trying to collect money from passersby. "It's a wonder we didn't get asphyxiated because we walked right behind the ambulance," she jokes.

Tony Scozzafava recalls they played behind Jerry's field off Green Street. "I remember E.F. Drew would dump their waste and – to get a ball – I would go to the dump and it would smell awful. It is a wonder I don't light up right now."

Mr. Basch delivered "live" fish on William Street every Thursday and Ms. French always got filet. Mr. Basch would clean the fish and we kids loved it.

There was an unspoken rule. People minded their own business. Asking personal questions to a neighbor or even a close friend was considered taboo.

Danny Bonanni remembered that the Giant Market located on Main Street and Division had a big fire in 1954. One night he came out of the State Theater after seeing a movie and Danny and his buddies climbed into his car. "I said to them that must be some fire at the Giant Market because I can still smell it up here." Then he looked around and realized it was his car that was on fire.

People had nicknames back in the 1930s and 1940s. Stanley Venturini was called "Stosh." Bill Bednar was called "Snagger" because if someone threw a ball near him he would always snag it. Other names remembered were T-Ball, Fonzi, Rudy Toody and Old Tipperary.

Everyone remembers you'd get a good shoe shine from Val Onorati.

Our oldest interviewee at 105, Ann Osterhoudt smiled as she said, "I remember a policeman – Gilmartin. He was a good guy. He was Chief of Police. He was old!!" When Lloyd and I came across an old picture with identifying names under the picture and saw Chief of Police Gilmartin, we were so excited.

Doris Hornick thought the boy who worked in Makovsky's Butcher Shop on Boonton Avenue was very handsome. She described him as having "rosy cheeks, black wavy hair and he looked beautiful wearing his white jacket!" (She married Marty Hornick soon after the end of WWII.)

Doris Hornick remembers that the Pilgrim Apartments were originally named the Darress Arms (and I think the building was done by the same investors who built the Darress Theater in the 1920s).

On the first floor of the Pilgrim Apartments they installed a tea room where lunch was served by waitresses, including a 17 year old Julia Dunn, who were dressed as pilgrims. Eventually, the tea room was closed and from that time until now, three different doctors have used that space for their offices. Currently the space is occupied by Dr. Moya-Mendez.

Ernestine Cascella told of how Dr. Musetto's wife was sick and Ernie's grandmother suggested to Dr. Musetto that Ernie could go over to their house and do some light dusting for them. "I can remember I was about 8 years old and they gave me 25 cents and I sat down and ate macaroni for dinner with them."

The Darress Theater had six dressing rooms. On the outside of the building, there is a panel on the left which is hinged. The panel was opened for animal acts when the theater was having a vaudeville show. They truck would pull up to the curb and the animals would walk the gangplank onto the stage.

Bill Nikel said that during the War it was difficult to get Fuller Brush men so they hired him as a Fuller brush "boy." Bill said he loved the experience.

Tony Scozzafava remembers a man coming to the school looking to hire kids to help pick strawberries because there was a shortage of men to do the work due to the War.

Bob Banks remembers a story about riding his new bike. "I rode my bicycle out to where my mother worked in Mountain Lakes and on the way back with the brand new bike I got stopped by the police. Nothing happened," he said, but Bobby realizes now that the police had stopped him because he was black and he was riding through a predominantly white neighborhood on a brand new bicycle.

Segregation in the 1930s and 1940s was the rule and, like a traffic light, people obeyed the rules and didn't question the validity or purpose of the rules. Black folks had their own community club called the Star Social Citizens Club. Bobby Banks remembered playing baseball for the Star Social Club and they always had a friendly rivalry with the Riverside Athletic Club. The Riverside AC met in an old building by the Rockaway River near Lake Avenue and played ball in the West Boonton ball park. It was very common in Boonton for people of different ethnicities to live in different parts of town.

One person – Mary Carmen – who was brought up in the 1920s recalls that she and her husband always went and sat in the back of the bus where black people were required to sit. She remembers her husband saying, "Those people do not deserve to be treated so unfairly."

Most people didn't pay attention to the issue of race. Even though the high school quarterback, Elmer Simms, was the star of the team, Worman's ice cream store would not serve him because he was black. A few of his teammates went with him to Lloyd's dad's store for ice cream because his dad always welcomed them. As Jim McGlone said it, "We were just dumb but we didn't think in terms of prejudice."

Women were excluded from important positions in the business world. Ann Reeves tells the story about winning a scholarship to a fashion school in New York City, and then becoming one of two finalists for a job at Vanity Fair magazine, "But they took the other girl because I was engaged and they figured I'd go and get married, get pregnant and quit."

53

Question?   And were they right?

ANN: Yes. If you wanted to have a 'career' you didn't get married.'"

There was a youth group formed at the Presbyterian Church called the PYADS, Presbyterian Young Adults. The group went to plays and movies together, and Sunday night they sometimes had supper together at the church. It was a good way for young people to meet and get to know each other. I mention this group because Lloyd was a PYAD and his acting career was launched and quickly ended with his one performance in a murder mystery production.

Speaking of Presbyterian Church, Lloyd has been a member lo these past 83 years. I joined the Church when I came to Boonton because of the camaraderie

Talking about performing, Jim McGlone remembers he was six years old when he was in his first performance in a production put on by Father Murphy at the Catholic Church. He also recalls being in a Minstrel Show put on by the Elks Club. And as an adult he joined the Mountain Lakes Dramatic Guild. That group is still in existence today and is thriving as *The Barn Theater* located on Skyline Drive in Montville, NJ.

Paul Werner told a story about when the trolley tracks were removed and Main Street repaved. "I remember Mr. Zangara had a market there and he was so frustrated when the street was closed for two or three weeks he planted a Victory garden in the middle of the street."

Near Lake Intervale someone remembers there was a "still" run by a man called Mr. McDonald.

Edith Bonanni Bacchetta was the young lady who sold movie tickets at the State Theater. After she graduated high school, Gilda Miccione took over that job and had it for many years.

Lou Squillace pumped gas while wearing a sports jacket.

There was an A&P located on Main Street which later moved to Washington Street. The store had a big fire when it was on Washington Street.

Bill Bednar remembers building bonfires at Hillary's Pond on New Year's Eve.

Fishing (permit required) is still something people enjoy in Boonton. Frank Wiswall remembers, "I sawed a broom handle and whittled both ends so it would work – and we'd go up to the Reservoir."

Before 1928, the movies were 'silent' movies and a few of the people we interviewed remembered going there. A well-dressed elderly man would walk down the aisle and sit in front of the piano. That signaled the movie would be starting and he would play appropriate music for each part of the movie. One friend recalls they were watching a cowboy movie and his friend kept yelling at the movie screen, "Look behind you – Look behind you." He was so engrossed in the story he had forgotten it was just a movie.

In a time before television, Saturday afternoon was spent at the State Theater eating popcorn and watching a serial story! A serial story was a short film maybe 10 minutes long, usually about Tarzan or cowboys, that was presented in 'chapters' that would go on for 13 weeks. Then there would be cartoons, like Mickey Mouse which was followed by a newsreel, then 'coming attractions' and finally a full length movie feature – anything from "Gone with the Wind" to western movies about people like Hopalong Cassidy or Gene Autry.

Don Estler loved going to the movies and he recalls that if you went to see all 13 chapters of a serial movie you would be given a new card with a punch on it so you could go to see the first chapter of the new series for free. After the movies Don and friends would go home by going through Grace Lord Park. Don recalls they would act out the parts of the movie with one friend acting the role of Buck Jones, while another would act the part of the bad guy, etc. Since hobos sometimes slept at the remains of the iron factory ovens nearby, "One day a hobo came stumbling out of the ruins and the boys got so scared they didn't stop running until they got home."

Cars were a luxury item and not many families owned one. In fact people did a lot of walking and did all of their shopping in neighborhood stores. In the 1920s trolleys came to Boonton bringing lots of people from neighboring towns to shop in Boonton and to see the local theaters – the Lyceum, the Boonton Opera House, and the State Theater. Boonton had bakeries, beauty shops, candy stores, car dealerships, drug stores and department stores like Boonton's Men's Shop, Willie Frankel's Men Shop, Zucker's, Newberry's 5 & 10, The Laurie Shop, Woolworth's 5 & 10 and Kottlers.

There was a furniture store, lots of grocery stores and meat and fish markets, soda fountains, jewelers, newspaper stores, paint stores, 3 or 4 hardware stores, pool halls, shoe repair, shoe shops, sporting goods shop and a Western Union office.

Talk to anyone in Boonton who grew up in the 1930s and 1940s and they will say with enthusiasm how much fun it was to go ice skating at Hillary's Pond, Sunset Lake, Lake Intervale, the Pond Bridge and Tumble Inn.

Ice skating was free, it was fun and in those days – before the invention of television - everyone went outside to do things like go ice skating or play ball. Bill Bednar remembers his brother telling him that he could ice skate all the way on the Morris Canal to Paterson, NJ.

Bobby Banks remembers "You could ice skate right on Plane Street."

Betty Bandura said, "I could skate from directly outside my house right over to Sunset Lake."

"Swimming?" The answers always include:

> The Basin and Deep Hole
> Sunset Lake
> Clay Hole
> Sandy Bottom
> Chestnut Street
> Pond Bridge
> Lake Avenue by the River
> Monroe Street near the old Silk Mill
> Ted Witty's place with the diving board

Bill Tredway, a volunteer fireman for 57 years, and a longstanding member of the ambulance squad, told us that over the years as many as 10 or more people died after diving into Deep Hole (which was below the Falls in Grace Lord Park). He recalled, "One mother was threatening to jump into the pool if the town didn't fill in Deep Hole." Eventually the town had to blast Deep Hole.

A big highlight of the late 1930s was the semi-pro football team in Boonton called The Boonton Panthers. The Panthers played football teams from Paterson and Newark. We heard many times that there was one year when the Panthers went the entire season without being scored upon!!!

One of the heroes of boxing fans was heavyweight boxing champion Joe Louis who retained his title from 1937 to 1949. Bobby Banks told us a story that all the kids would be playing on Plane Street until the boxing match was about to be broadcast on the radio. Then the street would empty out. After the fight -- and Joe Louis always won -- everybody would be back into the street screaming with excitement and elation.

Eleanor Higgins recalls, "I was a great Yankee fan. I used to go to the game by myself and I would get in for $.70 cents on 'lady's day.' I would go to double headers and not get home until 10 p.m."

Eleanor remembers that her Aunt Janet Taylor was a florist with a shop at 516 Main Street.

Bill Bednar remembers when he first went on the Police Department he was issued a badge and gun and he had to provide his own uniform.

Baseball star Lou Gerhig played baseball while he was in Columbia University under the name of Lou Long so he wouldn't lose his amateur standing. He played for a Morristown team that came to West Boonton Ball Field.

In 1940 the Kenvil, NJ Hercules Powder Company exploded. Lloyd said that one of his neighbors from Chestnut Street worked in the building where the explosion originated. That day he had to go to another building for something and so he was walking away from his building when it blew up. The force of the explosion knocked him flat on the ground but luckily he was not seriously hurt. See: http://www3.gendisasters.com/new-jersey/1946/kenvil,-nj-hercules-powder-company-explosion,-sept-1940.

Puddingstone is a type of rock that is prevalent in Boonton and it was Lloyd's wife Ann's favorite rock so he used it for her headstone in the cemetery.

SLEIGH RIDING

If you ever run out of conversation with someone who grew up in Boonton, just ask, "Where did you go sleigh riding?"

Lloyd remembers that he and his brother Jack, "We'd start at about Rockaway Street and we would go down Essex Avenue and make the turn toward the Pond Bridge but you'd have to stay way over near the curb because cars would be going down West Main Street. My dad once told me that he when he was a young boy in the early 1900s, he went sleigh riding down Boonton Avenue. When he got to Main Street he went over to Plane Street and ended down by the freight house on Morris Avenue. What a ride!"

Edna Austin loved sledding, "We'd go on William Street where there are steps that go down the steep hill and that's called Bunkety Hill and that is where we went sleigh riding."

Bobby Banks said, "The best sleigh riding was on Plane Street. The town did not sand or plow the streets back then. I got a Flexible Flyer sled for Christmas – the Cadillac of sleds – and we could go down Plane Street and up around Morris Avenue!"

Bill Bednar told me, "Duke Endrell would light the lanterns down by the railroad station on Birch Street because there was a lot of kids sleigh riding."

Fran Gibian went down Grant Street and Harrison Street. "They used to block off some of the streets like Wootton Street."

Ruth Halstead said she never went sleigh riding because it was too cold "and that's the truth!" She remembers that the town would close off Grant Street and Old Boonton Road and the kids would sleigh ride there.

Fred Ludwig still owns his Flexible Flyer. "We would sleigh ride down Bull Estler's hill. We called it Cow Hill behind the Park House" (which is now the location of Michelangelo's Restaurant).

Charlie Marshall (who grew up square dancing at the Marshall Barn) lives on Oak Road and said, "I could get to Powerville Road! You had to zigzag because you'd go so fast you could kill yourself." He could take his sled from his home on Oak Road and go all the way over to Ted Witty's place!

Harry Reeves said "Sleigh riding? I loved it! At night we used to sleigh ride on Chestnut Street and during the day we went up behind the Park House (Cow Hill)."

Lucille Scerbo loved sleigh riding and going down Liberty Street hill. "They never cleaned the streets off so it was packed and everything. My older brother went down Spruce Street. Now that's a long run from up at the top all the way down Spruce by the railroad! He was on a toboggan. We didn't have traffic like you have now."

Frank Wiswall loved this topic. "I used to love to sleigh ride. We didn't have to worry about cars on the road. Oh the fun we had on Spruce Street. That's a long ride. We'd have a kid at the bottom to watch for traffic. Only twice in 10 years did we see a car! We'd start at Green Street. There was always a lot of snow."

Eleanor Higgins recalls, "The Richards family had a bobsled and my mother used to say they used to go from Gaylord's Gate (that is way up Boonton Avenue) and go down Boonton Avenue and down to Scerbo Auto!" That's where the Boonton Avenue Grill is located today. But then, as Eleanor pointed out, "They had to walk all the way back up the hill!"

"Sleigh riding?" said Tony Scozzafaza, "We went to the top of St. Mary's Cemetery and we would come down through the cemetery on to Green Street and end up down around Boyle Street. Every once in a while when the conditions were perfect we would be able to go up to the top of Cedar then -- down Cedar, down Boonton Avenue - to Main Street. Or we used to go in the woods above Sunset Lake and you could come down through the woods and on to the Lake when it was frozen."

OTHER ACTIVITIES

Dancing was another enjoyable pastime for Boontonites. There were 'noon time dances' at Boonton High School and it was great fun to do the Jitterbug, Lindy, Cha Cha, Merenge, Samba, Rumba, Polka, Shuffle or Slow Dance. Things like the Twist and Hip-hop weren't part of our generation. We liked to hold the person with whom we danced.

There was "The Cross Club" at the old school building at Mt. Carmel Catholic Church, and on Friday night Doris Hornick, a pianist we interviewed, played live music with the "All American Girl Band" (young men were in the military at that time). They were chaperoned dances for teenagers that were held in the unused school building (which was eventually torn down to become a church parking lot). The girls who attended the dances liked to wear baggy sweaters, pleated skirts and penny loafers.

Bill Bednar was a great dancer and he remembers winning $1 in a dance contest at the Elks Club. Steve and Emily Bolcar remember meeting each other at the Sokol Hall dance and falling in love over 60 years ago.

Over at the old school building at Mt. Carmel during the War years, Father Murphy invited all the neighborhood kids to participate in activities such as basketball, ping pong and shuffleboard. The American Legion put on a Minstrel Show at Mt. Carmel, too.

When Lloyd was a young man, he and some friends would rent canoes at Decker's (located by the Powerville Dam) and bring along the fixings for a picnic and paddle upriver to the Boonton Wells.

A popular activity through from the 1940s to the 1960s was going to Marshall's Barn Dance on Oak Road. Charlie Marshall remembers that his dad would invite women to go square dancing for free while the men had to pay $.75! He said if the women are there the men would pay to come in.

ARRIVING AT THE SENIOR CITIZEN YEARS

Let's start with the 'worst' part of being a senior citizen. Mostly, the people we asked just laughed and said, as Ann Reeves did, "The Golden Years? Who are they kidding?"

Complaints included, "I can't clean the gutters anymore!"

Alice said, "I can't wear high heels anymore!"

"I can't move around as fast."

"When passing a mirror I am surprised at the person looking back."

"It is very lonely when a mate dies."

"Health concerns happen more often now."

"It is hard to watch friends suffer and die."

"I have to hold the banister now."

As Lloyd's dad Frank Charlton used to say, "Getting old ain't for sissies."

NOW FOR THE BEST SIDE OF BEING A SENIOR CITIZEN!!!!

Every day is a vacation day!

Not getting stuck in traffic on the way to work feels wonderful!

There is a sense of peacefulness that happens when you are no longer responsible for everything.

If your spouse is still with you, there is a joy every day in having a leisurely breakfast together.

Senior discounts and handicapped parking stickers are great!

We brag about our kids so much they would blush if they heard us.

Added to that – our grandchildren! They are perfect.   To hear a grandchild say, "Thank you, Grandma / Granddaddy. I love you!" That feeling is priceless!

Vacations! Dare I admit how many trips Lloyd and I have taken? We have known each other for over a dozen years and we have been on well over 125 trips at last count ---all out-of-state and varying from long weekends to several weeks. It is just plain fun to be retired, have a little extra money, enjoy good health and take time to travel to national parks, different countries and to visit friends who live near and far away.

Common statements we heard in every interview included:

> I am so fortunate!
> I am so blessed.
> I am so grateful.
> I feel so very lucky!

Well, Al and Grace we hope you've enjoyed our trip down memory lane! It is an honor to count ourselves as part of a generation of men and women – brought up in a time of great hardship – who managed to live lives of integrity, kindness, courage and character.

We are a generation where conscience is our hallmark and values are our compass. We are people who made a difference in the 20th century and because of us the world is just a little bit better!

Love – Lloyd and Terry

RADIO

Radio played a big part in our lives. Fred Ludwig said he and his friends would be playing stick ball in front of the Cullen house. At 7:30 p.m. they would stop their game and go over to where the Cullen's lived and sit on the porch and listen together to *The Lone Ranger* on the radio every Monday, Wednesday and Friday evening.

One program that I always enjoyed was called Edgar Bergen and Charlie McCarthy. Edgar was a ventriloquist and Charlie, his wooden dummy, was supposed to be a young boy with a sharp wit. A routine would sound like this:

W.C. Fields talking to the wooden dummy, Charlie

"Quiet, Wormwood, or I'll whittle you into a venetian blind."

Charlie": "Ooh, that makes me shutter!"

Or another joke

W.C. Fields: "Why, you stunted spruce, I'll throw a Japanese beetle on you."
Charlie: "Why you bar-fly, I'll stick a wick in your mouth and use you for an alcohol lamp!"

Or
W.C. Fields: "Step out of the sun, Charlie. You may come unglued."
Charlie: "Mind if I stand in the shade of your nose?"

*Some memorable **radio shows** we remember are:*

All Baseball Games!!!!
A Date with Judy
Abbott and Costello
Amos and Andy
Arthur Godfrey
Believe it or Not
Bing Crosby
Bob and Ray Show
Bob Hope
Boston Symphony
Buck Rogers in the 25th Century
Burns and Allen, George and Gracie
Can You Top This?
Death Valley Days
Duffy's Tavern
Edgar Bergen and Charlie McCarthy
Ellery Queen
Everrready Hour
Father Knows Best
FBI in War and Peace
Fibber McGee and Mollie
Fireside Chats
Fred Allen Show
Fred Waring Show
Gangbusters
George Jessel Show
Great Gildersleeve
Guy Lombardo Show
Helen Hays Theater
Henry Morgan Show
I Love a Mystery – with its squeaky door

It Pays to be Ignorant
Jack and Lena
Jack Armstrong
Jack Benny
Jimmy Durante
Joe Louis – boxing matches
Karl Hass Musicologist
Let's Pretend
Little Orphan Annie
Major-Bows Amateur Hour
Mert and Marge
Milton Berle
Monsignor Sheen
Ozzie and Harriet Nelson
Phantom
Sam Spade
Sunday Afternoon Opera
Sunday Afternoon American Radio
Warblers
Superman
Tarzan
Tennessee Jed Sloan
The Answer Man
The Cisco Kid
The Falcon
The Halls of Ivy
The Lone Ranger
The Green Hornet
The Judy Canova Show
The Moylan Sisters (they were only 5 and 7 years old!)
The $64 Dollar Question
Tom Mix
Truth or Consequences
War of the Worlds – with Orson Wells

TEACHERS IN BOONTON

Ms. Allen Biology

Mr. Benson Geometry

Ms. Blanchard English

Mr. Caplinger Science

Mr. Champion Arithmatic
         and School Principal

Ms. Coe

Ms. Combs Kindergarten

Ms. Cowen Bookkeeping

Ms. Carrie Davidson 2nd Grade

Ms. Jennie Davidson 2nd Grade

Ms. Emily Davis 5th Grade

Ms. Dennison (Ms. Spender)

Ms. Pearl Edmonds English

Ms. Edwards

Mrs. Erwin (was Ms. Jeffrey)

Ms. Hough 1st Grade

Ms. Kelsey Spelling

Ms. Kowal Bookkeeping

Ms. Leonard History

Mr. Mann   English/Superintendent

Ms. Maraziti English

Ms. Morrissey 2nd Grade

Ms. Marilyn Myers

Ms. Parsons Typing

Ms. Perone

Mr. Rott English

Ms. Schaumberg 2nd Grade

Mr. Kiefer Schriner Gym

Ms. Nancy Sinclair French

Ms. Spender 3rd Grade
         and then Kindergarten

Mr. Herbert Spurway Math –

(he had a disability)

Mr. Stengo Math

Ms. Sutton Math

Ms. Teague English

Ms. Vreeland Geometry

Ms. Wagoner Algrebra

Mr. Warford Music

Mr. Wittman Physics

Ms. Wicks 4th Grade

Dr. Wiggins School Doctor

Ms. Wilcox Commercial

Ms. Wootton Penmanship
         and School Principal

HERE'S A LIST OF STORES PEOPLE REMEMBER

A&P
Adams, Carson haircuts
Albrechti Diner
Alsterr's Deli & Liquor
Andy Sables Florist
Applegate Esso
Army and Navy Store
Arri Lorenzi
Avalone Barber Shop
Bachman Shoe
Baginski Junk Shop
Band Box Cleaners
Barbagallo's Groceries
Bartons Hardware Store
Bednar's Groceries
Bell Labs
Ben Segal
Berry Husky Bakery
Bill Baginsky
Block's Market
Bob's Men's Shop
Boonton Auto Parts
Boonton Bldg & Loan
Boonton Molding
Boonton Morristown Exp.
Boonton National Trust
Boonton Sweet Shop
Boonton Trust Company
Boontonware
Brady's Candy Store
Burnett & Hillary Used Cars
Carson Adams
Castaways
Cecil's Hair
Charlton Oil
Charretts Paper Store
Chiani Body Shop

Chinese Laundry
Christensen Gulf Gas
Cliff Smith Sports Shop
Cohen's Hardware
Colonial Bake Shop
Community Medical Group
Cohen's Hardware
Cork Factory
Cornelia St. Drug Store
Corriels
Corvi Soda Shop
Cozy Corner (actual Spelling was Kozy Korner)
Cowens
Cratura Pool Hall
D'Ello
Daisey Padavano Store
Darress Camera Store
Darress Theater
Dave Weinstein Papers
Dawson Lumber
Del Signore Market
Dixon Brothers
Dixon Funeral Home
Doland Machine
Doland Repair
Doll Factory
Doremus blacksmith
Drew, E.F.
Dunlap Tire
Edwards & Gifford Shoe
Edwards Pool Parlor
Elks Club
Emmons Blanchard Auto
Ernie Naas Garage
Esso
Excellent Candy

Ferris
Fish Furniture
Fisher Gas Station
Florence Beauty
Foncy Acoline taxi
Frankel Men's Shop
Friery's Cookerroo playground
Galloways
George Green Gas Station
George Morse Real Est.
George Price Market
George Shaw Saloon
Giant Supermarket
Gregory Grocery
Grobois Shoe Store
Hagen Bottling
Hennions Home & Barn
Henry's Liquor
Herman Smith Barber
Hitchcock Stationary
Holmes Library
Homeric Bldg & Loan
Hope Beauty Shop
Hurley's Pharmacy
Jacob Tredway & Sons
Janet Taylor Flower Shop
Jansen
Jean Adams Bake Shop
Jersey Bell
Jersey Central Appliance
Joe Torrisi
Johnny's Bar
Karp, Bill Appliance
Kelly Law Office
Kendells

Kimble Taxi
Kottler's Department Store
Kozy Korner
L. Ben Chinese
Lambiasi
Laurenzi, Ari Gift Shop
Lewis & Doyle
London's Grocery
Lou Mazzi
Louis Squallace
Lyceum Theater
Main Street Deli
Makovsky's
  Butcher Shop
Manfredonia
Maxfield Fire House
McCluskey
McCormick Bakery
McCormick's Tavern
Macollino
Makoski Butcher
Marcello
Martancik
Morris Kahn
Morris Marrone
Morse
Nugent
O'Hagen
Patty & Eddie
Phil's Flower Shop

Provost Taxi
Punch & Judy
Ralph & Toots
Ratti's Soda Fountain
RI Heath Harness
Robierios
Royal Scarlet
Sabatino Market
Sabol's Meat Market
Saul NYCE Paint Store
Scerbo Pontiac
Scerbo Grocery
Schnable Jewelry
Segal, Ben Shoe Shop
Shirley Shop
Shoprite
Simpson Candy Store
Siromas
Smith (Cliff) Sports Shop
State Theater
Steve Colvin Jewelry
Sulzberger Ford
Sunshine Bakery
Telfer Beer Garden
Thodes Soda Shop
Times Bulletin Newspaper
Tody Tedesco Veg Market
Tom O'Grady Grocery

Tony's Barber Shop
Tracy Fish Market
Trail's End Pet Supply
Tredway Express
Tredwayand Case Grocery
Van Raalte
Vanderhoof, Reg
VanDynes Machine Shop
Venturini's Deli
Verdi's Shoe Store
Walt Sikora Paper Store
Weinberg Chemicals
Wendt Photo Studio
Western Union
Whalen Drug Store
White Way
Woolworth 5 &10
Worman Ice Cream
Worman's Liquor
Wrights Aero
Zandell Shoe Store
Zeidman's Cleaners
Zucker Shoe Store
Zucker Dept. Store

On the following three pages you will find some of the paintings by Bob Bogue in black and white. These and others by him are available in full color in the book:

THE ARTISTRY OF BOB BOGUE by Lloyd Charlton

This book is available at the Historical Society Museum gift shop.

Paintings by Bob Bogue
- Boonton Churches -

Methodist Church on Main St.

New Methodist Church

First Presbyterian Church

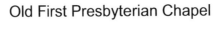

Old First Presbyterian Chapel

Mt. Carmel Catholic Church

Rockaway Valley Church

Bob Bogue's paintings
of a few of Boonton's older buildings

Puddingstone Inn

Train Station

Maxfield Fire House

Salmon Lumber

State Theater

Historical Society Museum
formerly the John Taylor Building

Bob Bogue's paintings
of some of Boonton's older buildings

1 Cornelia Street House
2 Holmes Library
3 Lower Main Street
4 Trolley on Main St.
5 Kozy Korner
6 Boonton High School
7 Park House – now
Michelangelo's Restaurant

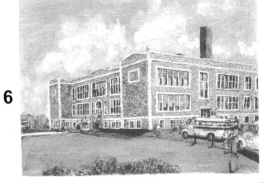

Drawings by Margot Durrer's friend Edna about WWII

Here she is making fun of
1- being out of gas
2 - rubber shortage
(saving tire in the safety deposit box)
3 - offering guest "one sugar or none"

4 - Edna drops food and runs outside
To be an air raid warden
5 - "Our friend the oil man" with the dog
acting friendly to him (oil was rationed)

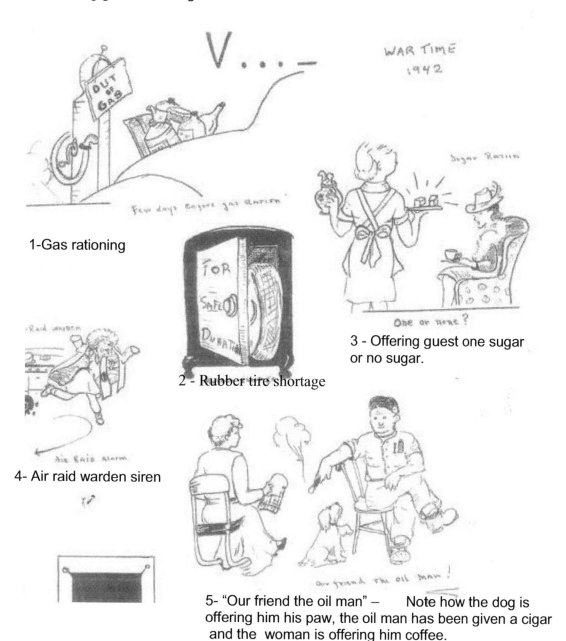

1-Gas rationing

2 - Rubber tire shortage

3 - Offering guest one sugar or no sugar.

4- Air raid warden siren

5- "Our friend the oil man" –   Note how the dog is
offering him his paw, the oil man has been given a cigar
and the woman is offering him coffee.

Some things we did growing up in Boonton

Fishing

Swimming at Ted Witty's

Hiking in Tourne

Ice Skating at Pond Bridge

Renting a canoe at Decker's

Swimming at the Falls

Marshall's Barn

Go-cart racing

Boonton's Centennial 1967

To honor our predecessors at Boonton's Centennial in 1967, a lot of men in town became "Brothers of the Brush" and grew beards.

Fred Ludwig (far left) looked so good as a "Brother" he is still wearing his beard in 2010. Can you guess who he resembles?

Familiar scenes in town

The Arch Bridge

Octagonal House built 1850s

Post Office on Main St. as of 2010

National Bank Building was originally a 2-story building. Look closely to see the line where new bricks were added.

Pilgrim Apts. Church & Birch Streets. Built circa 1930s, this photo was Taken in 2010

VFW Post 242

Grace Lord Park

Aerial view of Boonton

Familiar scenes in town

Boonton's Town Hall in 2010

BELOW -- The Prall House was the first house in Morris County that had electric lights. It was designed so that one switch would put on the lights in the entire house! Electricity was such a novelty that people would gather in front of the house waiting for Mr. Prall to come home and throw the switch.

Darress Theater
owner Tom Timbrook

Memorial Day

Every year on Memorial Day the town folk come together to honor the men and women in the military who gave their lives so that the United States of America will always be free.

The name of each Boonton person who died in military service during the last century is read. Wreaths are presented by various groups and churches in town, and three gun shots ring out in memory of the brave servicemen who died to keep us free.

Memorial Day

Al Scerbo was in the Pacific in the 6th Marine division and was assigned to amphibian tanks. The Marines were his pride and joy and he was an active member of the VFW and he was Post Commander of the American Legion.
Until his recent death, Al headed the Memorial Service every year.

Al Scerbo

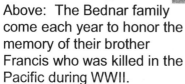

Above: The Bednar family come each year to honor the memory of their brother Francis who was killed in the Pacific during WWII.

Ann Reeves, a folk artist in New Jersey, painted this picture in 2008, reflecting her memories of Boonton's Memorial Day. Look carefully on the right are Boy Scouts and Girl Scouts putting flags on the graves in the cemetery for the people who served in the military.

Firemen's Labor Day Parade

As Boonton's Harmony Drum Corps approach the Reviewing Stand, they fan out on either side of the street. The Color Guard marches down the middle of Main Street. Then the firemen march forward and salute as they approach the Reviewing Stand.

Firemen's Carnival
Labor Day Weekend

State Senator Tony Bucco,
Congressman Rodney Freylinghausen,
Assemblyman Rick Merkt.

The Fire Department offers free hotdogs
and a drink immediately after the Labor
Day parade.

Alex Paulozzo and Zachary Johnson,
grandsons of two long time leaders of
Harmony Drum Corps, take part in the
Harmony concert at the Carnival.

Bridget and Jackie on the giant slide.

Harmony Drum Corps performing at Carnival.

A family at the Carnival.

Halloween

The van decorated to resemble a TANK was the idea of my son Bill and his wife Adrienne – with the help of many friends!

Boonton Township has a 'tailgate' party on Halloween often with live music.

Colleen and Dr. Sharon Burke with their nieces Bridget and Jackie – our granddaughters.

Terry Nanny made her granddaughters matching "Pilgrim" outfits.

We saw this 'hot dog' on Halloween!

Harmony Drum Corps parade down Main Street on Halloween wearing Halloween costumes.

Main Street Org. - Holiday Activities

Lighting up Main Street for the Holiday season!

Harmony performs!

Holiday carriage rides provided by Main Street Org.

SCOUTING IN BOONTON

Scouting began in February 1910 and the Boy Scouts of America celebrated their 100th anniversary in February 2010. The first troop in Boonton started in September 1910 and has been continuously in operation for 100 years. They celebrated this achievement with an exhibit in the Boonton's Historical Society Museum.

Above is the Scouting Float in the Boonton Santa Parade in November 2010.

The above photos of the Boy Scouts and Girl Scouts dates back to the 1970s when Lloyd's children were in scouting. The patches show 48 consecutive Klondike Derbys and date back to 1955.

84

ROTARY CLUB OF BOONTON

The Boonton Rotary contributes to Rotary International. Locally, it provides several high school scholarship awards. It also donates dictionaries and Thesaurus books to all third and fourth graders in the schools of Boonton, Boonton Township and Mountain Lakes, among its other charitable works.

Paul Wilson, past President of Boonton Rotary, in 2005 photographing a child for Kid Care identification which Rotary does every year on Community Day.

Congressman Freylinghausen visits Rotary

In 2010, Rotary provided a needed fence to a local preschool

Fundraising activities

.Main Street has Community Day every September

On Community Day a part of Main Street is closed to traffic and the town businesses and local organizations are encouraged to set up a table to display what they do. Various groups perform. .

Here's our church choir, First Presbyterian Church, in September 2010

Here comes Harmony performing on Community Day!

The Historical Society participates   Here's a future "Harmony performer!

The Santa Parade – the Saturday after Thanksgiving

The Saturday after Thanksgiving we have a Santa Parade that is televised on our local cable channel. It's a short parade that ends at Santa Land. On the left is a photo of Historical Society members dressed in period clothing.

The New Horizon Band features only 'senior citizens.'
Lloyd took his first trumpet lesson at age 80 and that's him on the float! Boy were his fingers frozen!

Volunteers
Rockaway Valley Garden Club

Among other things, members of the Club plant and water some of the flowers you see in public spaces around town. They created the "Wildflower Trail" in the Tourne.

Yearly plant sale held the
Saturday before Mother's Day
In parking lot of Michelangelo's
Restaurant.

Some garden club members at the Wildflower Trail in the Tourne.

Making a water garden in Boonton Township.

Every year they single out and honor people who help the town –
Here they are honoring the Crossing Guard in 2004.

Volunteers

Meet Boonton's Mayor Cy Weklilski.

Trustees of the Boonton Historical Society when Lloyd was a Trustee.

Boonton volunteer firemen at a fire on Church Street in 2006.

In this car rescue, the fireman with the name "Charlton" on his jacket – he's Lloyd's son Bill.

In 1998, Lloyd was awarded this medal by District leadership for 50 years of service to the Cub Scouts and Boy Scouts.

Lloyd with sons Bill & Art

& with grandsons John and Joshua

89

Volunteers
Historical Society Activities

"High Tea" is a
yearly fundraiser.

"Cemetery" Talk –
Lloyd Charlton - represents his grandfather,
John Charlton, who was a soldier in the Civil War.

Lloyd's son Art Charlton (shown above)
is representing William Meadowcroft
who worked for Thomas Edison

Town Walks are given in different parts of town.
Lloyd hosts the 'Main Street' walk twice a year.

Special Memories

Nel Simms and Senator Dole

Best friends: Lloyd, Bob Bogue, Don Estler

Grand slam MVP – Grandson Nick

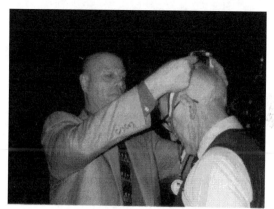

Former Mayor Ed Bolcar honoring Lloyd's
Army service in 1946.

Library dedication to Ann Charlton

Bret Schundler and Jane Hopkins

Special Memories

In 1936 Whitfield Estler was a young
Boy Scout when he died unexpectedly
at the age of 14.
Each year Don and Lois Estler participate
in a service held by Scouts of three towns
who come to honor Whitfield.
The ceremony was created by the
Rockaway Boy Scouts. Lloyd, as a Scout
Leader, marches silently behind the flag as
the Scouts enter the cemetery.

In 2006, when Pat Fowler turned 100,
she was named Grand Marshall at the
Santa Parade. Pat was a kindergarten
teacher for 50 years.

When the statue of the fireman holding the child was installed at the Firemen's Home, the Town
held a dedication ceremony several years ago.

ALPHABETICALLY SPEAKING

Adams, Gilda DeFiore	02/04/10
Austin, Edna Martin	11/02/09
Bacchetta Al and Edith	07/26/10
Bandura, Betty	04/12/10
Banks, Bobbie	01/21/10
Bednar/Bonanni/Tredway	10/05/09
Birch, Bill	03/26/10
Bogue, Bob and Lynn	01/02/10
Bolcar, Stephen	03/19/10
Bonanni, Danny (see Bednar)	10/05/09
Carman, Mary Leva	02/05/10
Cascella, Ernestine Prevost	12/17/09
Charlton Lloyd (see Estler)	12/08/09
Charlton, Robert	12/07/09
Condon, Al & Grace	07/28/10
Di Eduardo, Marie	04/07/10
Dunn, Julia	10/05/09
Durrer, Margo Ammann	01/17/10
Estler/Charlton Lloyd	12/08/09
Franchi, Gladys Bertell	11/30/09
Geier, Lee – Ltr	03/01/10
Gibian, Fran Smith	02/26/10
Halstead, Ruth	03/25/10
Heaton, Alice Charlton	12/31/09
Hezlitt, George and Dot	01/08/10
Higgins, Eleanor	04/01/10
Hornick, Doris Borgstrom	11/03/09
Ludwig, Fred	02/11/10
Marshall, Charlie	01/26/10
McCormick, Gloria Weiser	12/21/09
McGlone, Jim	07/18/10
Nikel, Bill	01/20/10
Osterhoudt, Ann Barnish	03/01/10
Perry, Asperina Croce	03/04/10
Reeves, Ann	04/09/10
Reeves, Harry	02/20/10
Scerbo, Lucille Hopkins	02/04/10
Scozzafava, Tony	07/29/10
Strelec, Joe	04/14/10
Tredway, Bill (see Bednar)	10/05/09
Werner, Paul	02/24/10
Wiswall, Frank and	02/09/10
Mae Beiermeister Wiswall	

ADAMS, GILDA (DE FIORE) -   Interview 02/04/10 – by Terry Charlton

I met her at the senior center meeting of the "Boontonites" where she volunteers as the secretary keeping the minutes of each meeting. She's trim, incredibly sweet and I believe there isn't a person who doesn't like her. In fact, if effervescence had a name, it would be Gilda DeFiore Adams, Boonton High School Class of 1943.

Her face lights up when she speaks – and she speaks a lot because her recall is phenomenal. In her mind's eye she sees the vendor carrying a bundle over his shoulder of fresh fish wrapped in newspaper and ice. She remembers, too, that during Prohibition – if you were Italian and needed the ingredients to make anisette - he would have just what you wanted hidden under the satchel of fish.

Siblings? There were Alfonse, Nonnie, Jenny, Louise and six years later Gilda. She was told her name was pronounced "JILL-DA" but when she attended public school the teachers called her Gilda. Coming to America from Italy, her father Carmen DeFiore made $11 every two weeks as a laborer at the DLW (Delaware Lackawanna) in Hoboken. She tells the story that her dad first settled in Montville and believed he was living in Oklahoma. There's a street in Montville that is now called Oklahoma.

"My oldest sister Nonnie – she had diphtheria" and luckily survived. Diphtheria was a potentially fatal disease of the nose, throat and air passages. Diphtheria was a leading cause of death among children.   The potential complications of diphtheria included the following: inflammation of the heart and congestive heart failure, muscle paralysis and vision problems, lung, blood and bone infection, and death.

On a happier note, although they didn't have much money for toys, Gilda still owns three of the dolls she received as a child. Gilda loved paper dolls, too, and with her unusually lucid memory she began reciting the names of the paper doll Dionne quintuplets – Emilie, Marie, Yvonne, Annette and Cecile.

Gilda doesn't remember having a birthday party as a child. So for her 80th birthday her children invited 80 guests and surprised her with a birthday party. "It was wonderful!"

Gilda enjoyed Halloween and tagged along after her older sisters. They stopped at a house of a person they called the "green monster." He was nasty and demanded, "Take your mask off" and Gilda's sister replied, "I'll take mine off if you take your mask off." We laughed and laughed. Then she also remembered the time when they were going to the English teacher's house, Mrs. Teague, and Mrs. Teague jumped out from behind a hedge and said, "I got you. It was so much fun. We laughed and laughed."

She remembers shopping for dresses to wear to school, and each day she would alternate between the two outfits she owned. She was so envious of classmate Jeannie because Jeannie had knee socks!

"They were very strict in the Methodist Church on Main Street," Gilda said as she remembered her friend Sarah. "Don't dance. Don't wear lipstick. You can't go to the movies on Sunday."

The State Theater was a wonderful way to spend a Saturday. In fact, Gilda loved Hopalong Cassidy. She even wrote to Bill Boyd and she received a signed picture. "I was thrilled."

When she was about 12, Gilda's mother died. Gilda told me, "In those days, you were waked in the house and today when I go into a flower store and I get that smell of roses – it all comes back." She recalls that no one comforted her. In fact, relatives from the Bronx came and reproached her for smiling during the wake. They told her to wear black and not play the radio for a year. Luckily, Gilda's father didn't require the children to follow that old fashioned Italian tradition. Their mother's death was suffering enough.

Gilda graduated high school 6th in her class and became a member of the National Honors Society. Having taken a commercial course in high school, she got a great job in New York City and her co-worker, Jack Adams, soon became her steady date. They were married in 1959 and within three years they had three children, John, Barbara and Jane. When the children reached school age she took a part-time job as a bookkeeper for Ari Laurenzi who had a gift shop of Main Street.

After only 30 years of marriage, Jack suffered a stroke and was ill for several years before succumbing to pneumonia.

I asked her what was hard about being a senior citizen. She said attending a 'couples' event like a wedding makes her feel lonely as she'd like to dance, too.

However, when her sister talks about sad memories, Gilda says, "Knock it off! Look ahead!" Gilda finds happiness with her cat "Elsa." She also loves shopping, going to the movies, enjoying her favorite programs on television, and visiting with friends, as well as participating in group activities. Frankly, as she put it – "I feel blessed. I don't get down." With Gilda's sunny disposition, you know that's a fact!

Or just maybe it is the legacy of having a Boonton childhood filled with lots of good friends, myriad new adventures and lots of laughter and fun!

AUSTIN, EDNA (MARTIN) -

Interview 11/20/09 – by Terry Charlton

Nicknamed "Edie," Edna Martin Austin was born in Morristown Memorial Hospital, the youngest of five children. Her mother died while giving birth to Edna and she was raised by Dolly and Robert Lucas, who were her guardians. They had five children ranging in age from 7 to 17 when she arrived at their home on William Street so she was destined to be spoiled with lots of love and attention. She remembers her only weekly chore was to dust the dining room for which she was paid 25 cents! With the State Theater costing 15 cents, and a Whelan's ice cream cone 5 cents, she felt rich!

Edna's house on William Street was one block from Main Street. Robert Lucas owned a butcher store on Main Street at Plane Street. Their 14-room house included a summer kitchen and a winter kitchen, they had a telephone as far back as she can remember and the family owned an automobile that was driven by their chauffeur when they took their regular Sunday afternoon outings. The family liked to holiday at the Jersey Shore and this is still one of Edna's favorite vacation spots.

Edna was a child who loved to play!!! One of her favorite memories was wheeling a doll carriage with her beautiful big doll inside around Main Street while wearing dress-up clothes she found in her parents' attic! She distinctly remembers at the corner of Birch and William Street there was a sewer drain and she would crawl into the drain and through the tunnel and come out on the other side of the street! She remembers putting an ironing board on the posts of a nearby house and using empty cans to play store. Edna remembers she was showered with lots of presents given to her by her Aunt Mable (her mother's sister) who was Lois Crane's mother (Lois married Don Estler).

Besides Lois (a/k/a Beansie), Edna played with Betty Hopkins and Dicky Davis. One game she remembers is sitting on the big steps of a home on William Street. She'd put a stone behind her back in one hand and then held out her fists so the person had to guess in which hand the stone was hidden. If the person guessed correctly, they could move up a step. There was a slate sidewalk nearby and she loved to roller skate on the slate, much to the chagrin of the neighbor. She loved ice skating at Sunset Lake and one of her favorite memories was Bunkety Hill where they went sleigh riding. That is a hill on William Street next to the 'William Street stairs" that lead down to Union and Division Streets.

Edna recalls fondly that one of her five cats, probably Casper Chinzy Herringbone, would climb up the tree, climb on the roof and then 'meow' at her bedroom window! Edna loved a radio program called "Little Orphan Annie" and would telephone her cousin Beansie to talk about the latest mystery on the show. Edna admits on Halloween she once put soft apples on the concrete porch of a neighbor and then stepped on the apples to be sure they were squishy as her 'mischief night' prank.

She had one teacher, Ms. Morrissey, who chided her for doing so poorly on a math quiz, and wrote on her paper, "Did you do this with your eyes closed?" Yet Edna was good enough at math to be given the high privilege of being the 'change' girl at Newberry's 5 and 10 cent store where she made change for other cashiers.

Edna met John Austin when she was a teenager attending the Presbyterian Church. She was 22 when they married and they honeymooned at Niagara Falls. As a newlywed, Edna's mother-in-law asked her what she was making for dinner and she replied, 'I am baking hotdog rolls because we are having hotdogs tonight." Obviously, Edna loved to cook because she was actually baking her own hot dog rolls!!! After two years of marriage, their daughter Jean was born and Jean has always been the light of her life. John worked in maintenance, and when Jean went to school, Edna got a job at Jersey Bell and retired from there 30 years later.

Edna remembers the time she thought she would be electrocuted. She had a spin-dry washing machine and once she touched the spigot and the vibrations froze her to it. She had the presence of mind to bend herself around and work the plug out of the wall. "I was very fortunate but it was the scariest time in my life."

Edna's hobbies were cooking, needlepoint and volunteering at the church. She and John also volunteered at The Castaways Shop, a second hand store that raised money for St. Clare's Hospital. She and John (who died in 2008) loved to travel and went to Europe, Hawaii, and Alaska and went on several cruises during their retirement years. She volunteers today and has been a charter member of the Presbyaires, a local singing group that began at the Presbyterian Church about 15 years ago. The group sings at nearby senior residences and at nursing homes.

I asked Edna if she experienced any challenges as a senior citizen and she smilingly replied, "Not a thing. It's fine. I have blossomed out now more than at any time in my life. I am a leader and I am enjoying it!"

BACCHETTA, AL & EDITH (BONANNI) - Interview 08/23/10 – by Terry Charlton

Al and Edith (Bonanni) Bacchetta grew up in Boonton. He became a carpenter and she became a legal secretary and, later on, she married Al and became the mother of two wonderful sons. They live in a beautiful home that Al built. They have been married over 60 years and several years ago they took their entire family of 14-1/2 people on a 9-day cruise to the Caribbean and Bermuda. They wore yellow t-shirts on the trip that read "Bacchetta Family Cruise."

Al and Edith say with genuine joy in their voices, "Best money we ever spent! The grandchildren are still talking about it."

Can one short paragraph capture the spirit of these two charming people? I think so. It's easy to see they are very family-oriented, fun-loving, kind, generous, thoughtful and happy people who believe in family values and commitment to the community. Bill's T-shirt displaying the American flag and his amazing War record attest to his patriotism. Al has been a volunteer fireman for 54 years and Edith has been right there with him as a member of the Women's Auxiliary.

"I was born on Morris Avenue," says Al. Morris Avenue went over the bridge that used to be there (before Route 287 was created) and under the trestle and around to Grace Lord Park. "It's now called Monroe Street."   Growing up with 7 siblings, "I am one of 51 grandchildren" Al boasts. Most of Al's relatives lived next door or across the street and that part of town was dubbed "Little Italy." Al was never short of friends to play with since so many cousins lived nearby.

His grandfather was a contractor who worked on building "the Boulevard" in Mountain Lakes.

Al recalls that once in a while several families would decide to go to Keansberg together for a day at the Shore. They would go in a convoy of 4 or 5 cars, all filled to overflowing with family. Al remembers their car had pull-up seats located in front of the back seats, so they could put 7 or 8 people in each car. It was a time before major highways or air conditioned cars, and the 30 mile trip took several 'long and hot hours.'

Edith's house as a young girl was on Boonton Avenue, then called Brook Street. She had an older sister and younger brother. As was the custom of the time, Edith got to wear her sister's 'hand-me-down' clothes. Like Al's family, Edith remembers her father raising chickens in the back yard.

Edith recalls fondly how much fun it was to cut out paper dolls from the newspaper and save them in a shoe box. When Edith was 8 years old she was in a car accident. She was not badly hurt but she had to go to the hospital. When she was recovering, "My parents gave me a little doll and she was my whole life!" Her mother generously gave the doll to some friends who were visiting with their little girls saying, "Edith is getting too big for the doll." Edith remembers, "My heart was broken. My mother apologized 1,000 times." Memories like that remind us that children are people, too, and need to be respected. In that era, children were not invited into decision-making.

Edith and Al describe their parents as being strict. You clearly knew what was expected of you and you never stepped over that line. A birthday treat would be buying a coconut layer cake from the Cottage Bakery! Bakery foods were a very rare family treat. Sundays after church there would be plenty of Italian dishes, like spaghetti and meatballs, for anyone who wanted to drop by for dinner. Al remembers how the old timers would sit around the dining room table with a glass of wine and some peanuts and talk for hours and hours. "Not like today,"Al muses. "When everyone finishes dinner, they rush to the TV to watch a ball game."

Al talked about 'bank night' at the State Theater. If you bought a movie ticket you would be entered into a drawing for a $100 prize. Lots of people came down to buy movie tickets, but not to see a movie. Many of the people would wait at the Three Links Hall located next door to the dentist, Dr. Bider's house, on Cornelia

Street. Once the winning number was announced over a loudspeaker, the young kids would ask the adults for the unused movie tickets and the kids would then go to see the 'second show' at the theater.

Edith worked as a cashier in the State Theater before Gilda Migioni. She remembered it was a fun job and a ticket cost 15 cents. "Tuesday night was dish night! Anyone buying a movie ticket was entitled to a free dinner plate or dish. It was a very busy night!"

Al served in the Army, joining in 1943. He was assigned to a medical outfit that was sent to France and then marched into Germany. He arrived in the Dachau concentration camp as a libertor in1945 just as the War in Europe ended. "It was really, really terrible. I can still see it in my mind today. We saw things that we couldn't believe. Bodies piled one on top of another. And the prisoners were very sick and they were so thin."

"Al," I asked in amazement, "Did it affect you?" Al response was immediate, "No. We had a job to do. We had to keep going and do what we could do." He faced an appalling situation with the maturity not usual in such a young man, and I was awed by his presence of mind. Since I have read stories about prisoners who were liberated at Dachau, I was thrilled to meet one of the Americans who actually brought medicine and hope to the prisoners who were incredulous and almost afraid to believe that their awful nightmare had actually ended.

On a brighter note, when Al met Edith after he returned from his military service he remembers that they went quickly from courtship to engagement, and then to a beautiful June wedding. As someone from another interview told me, "Everybody just wanted to get back to life the way it was before the War."

Following in his father's footsteps, Al became a union carpenter and was able to make a good living as he was very skilled. He said it was the custom at that time for a young man to follow in his father's trade and Al would have felt guilty if he followed his own fantasy, which had been to have a military career. Edith, on the other hand, adored her working career as a legal secretary and, in fact, she loved to spend a day a week helping out as a secretary at her son's law practice on Main Street.

During Al's career as a volunteer fire fighter, he worked at many fires, including the fire at Giant's Market, the White Way Diner, and at a fire with fatalities on Dorian Road. He continued, "I remember the fire at the Puddingstone Inn when it burned to the ground. It was so bitter cold I couldn't get warm for 2 or 3 days."

Asked about how they enjoy retirement, Edith is quick to respond, "We were able to retire at 62 and 63. We got to travel to Europe 3 or 4 times and took about 23 cruises." In fact, they told us that in a few weeks they will be going on vacation to Lancaster, Pennsylvania traveling with the Boontonites (a group formed in Boonton comprised of senior citizens who meet twice a month and often take trips together in the U.S. and abroad).

Edith loves simple things like her morning coffee at the dining room table while she reads the newspaper. She enjoys gardening and they have three bird houses in their yard so they can enjoy watching the birds through binoculars. "I have loved all the parts of my life," said Edith. "I loved being a mother. And now I love retirement!"

Al agreed saying, "You ask me what is the best part of being a senior? I wake up at 8 o'clock and ask myself if I want to get up yet – and then I say 'no.'"

Edith laughingly agreed, "We go at our own pace. We don't answer to anybody. The kids are grown and on their own. We love them and they come to see us often."

And then Al and Edith chime in together to a statement we have heard over and over in our interviews:

"We are so fortunate."

BANDURA, BETTY (SIKORA) - Interview 04/12/10 – by Terry Charlton

If there were a contest for a model senior citizen Betty would have to win because she has 'attitude' and what a wonderful attitude it is. Betty can tell you a story better than the comedian Bob Hope and when she smiles her face lights up and you find yourself laughing, too.

"I'm so lucky. I have a great life" she says with an energy in her voice that makes you believe she is telling you the truth.

Betty is still very active and runs the local "Thrift Shop" where she works Tuesday, Thursday and Saturday and all profits are donated to the Mt. Carmel Catholic Church.

Betty's dad worked for the railroad and rose to a high level of management. He walked with a cane and, in hindsight, Betty believes he probably had polio as a child. She also had two older sisters - Ann and Florence. When Betty was growing up, her teenage sister Florence died of tuberculosis. The loss left an indelible hurt still visible today when Betty talks about Florence. After Florence died, "They had to burn all our clothes" because tuberculosis was highly contagious." Betty remembers going to the cemetery where, every Sunday, music was played for one hour.

Surrounded by her Sikora extended family, she remembers that Uncle Walter ran 'Walt's Newspaper Store' on Main Street and worked 7 days a week for 50 years. Her grandma (whom she called by the Polish word "Prababka") lived nearby and she had a special Polish tradition of cooking and serving lots of food on Christmas Eve (one year Betty counted 18 different dishes lovingly prepared for a house full of people).

"Then at the end of the meal – this is so exciting – we'd have Communion wafers from the church and you would take it and say to the person beside you, 'I wish you happiness and good health.' Then that person took another Communion wafer to the next person and would repeat 'I wish you happiness and good health.' And it went all the way around the room."

When her parents returned from Midnight Mass on Christmas Eve, they would decorate the Christmas tree and put out gifts from Santa. "I will never ever forget Christmas!!! I wish we could do it again."

Being enrolled in St. John's School (now Wilson School), she had only three classmates –and they were all named Betty. At first the advanced level of school work was difficult but she soon learned to love it.

Asked to recall Boonton memories, Betty insists she actually went sleigh riding down Wootton Street. She describes how she could "Skate from my house on Oak Street to Sunset Lake" and she remembered a small building there at the lake where they sold hot chocolate. "Oh, I loved it!"

She loved it when Gloria McCormick's mother came by on Saturday with her bakery truck with wonderful things for sale. "She was a great baker!"

Another vendor who came to the door was the Hallocks (phonetic) who sold "tea and soaps."

When the truck came by selling 'live chickens' she'd call to her mother, "No chickens over here!" because she knew they would have to kill the chickens and that made her very upset.

Ever the tomboy, one Sunday walking home from getting the newspaper for her dad, Betty passed the back of the Lyceum Theater and saw a way to get inside. She went into what turned out to be dressing rooms and there on the wall was a flyer for the appearance of "George Burns." She found her way up to the actual stage, "And it was so beautiful. It was great!" Then she let herself out and went home with the newspaper.

Betty also recalled, "I remember as a child I would walk across the stage in the State Theater wearing my Halloween costume and they would give prizes."

Betty remembers as a child of 8 or 9 years old, a classmate died. Betty came home and said to her mother, "I have to wear a white dress and veil tomorrow because I am going to be a polar bear." Finally, Betty's mother figured out what she was talking about. Six little girls had been picked to walk down the church aisle beside her school friend's little white casket. She was a pallbearer.

Turning from a sad moment to a happier one, Betty remembers there was a boisterous commotion coming from Main Street on the day the Japanese surrendered and WWII ended, and she was trying to take a violin lesson. The teacher dismissed her instead and Betty ran down to Main Street and saw the excitement. "Boonton was going crazy! Everybody was kissing everybody. It was a great day."

After the War ended, Betty was working as a receptionist at Bell Labs and had to talk on the phone to the security department located at the other entrance to the building. The person she spoke to was Stanley Bandura and Betty fell in love with his voice and wanted to meet him. "His voice was so sincere, honest and kind!" So having first fallen in love over the phone, they soon started dating and two years later they were married. Stanley didn't talk about it often but during WWII while he was stationed in Italy his tank was attacked and everyone killed. He was able to crawl away from the tank because he knew if the Italian soldiers found him alive they would kill him. Eventually he was rescued and he had to spend two years in a hospital in New Jersey. Stanley was awarded the Purple Heart for being wounded in action.

Betty's believes her children Stanley and Dorie, and Stanley's family including her two teenager grandsons are her greatest treasures. She speaks with sadness that her husband Stanley died of cancer after only 18 years of marriage. If only he could see his children now and his grandsons how proud he would be!

Winding up our interview, I asked –

What gives you joy – not counting family or career?

Betty answered honestly   "Everything."

What's hardest about being a senior citizen? "Getting old!"

Betty, do you have any 'words of wisdom?'

   "KEEP LAUGHING."

      Thanks – that's a great motto!

"I am going to be very honest with you. When Lloyd Charlton called me up for this interview, had it not been for the fact that I was the first black Police Chief in the Town of Boonton, I don't think I would have done it but I felt a responsibility."

Bobby's mother was a very loving person and an exceptional role model for him. He was expected to do his share to help his family and he was taught to thank God by attending church. His mother also made sure he was well educated. That upbringing catapulted Bobby into becoming the first black Police Chief not only of Boonton but of Morris County.

Now it is Bobby who has become the role model – the person who makes us believe in possibilities. He is the kind of person you instantly like because he is both funny and insightful. He spoke frankly in the interview saying that he never really knew his dad and his mother worked as a domestic. Her work must have been quite outstanding as her employer in Mountain Lakes picked her up and brought her home.

Bobby does not remember receiving many toys growing up on Plane Street. When he was 12, he dreamed of receiving a bicycle for Christmas. On Christmas morning, he came into the living room and there was no bike. He shrugged his shoulders. He understood bikes were expensive. When his mother asked him to get her a drink from the kitchen, "Naturally I went to the kitchen and turned on the light – and there was the bike!"

Bobby remembers, "I rode my bicycle out there to where my mother worked in Mountain Lakes and on the way back with the brand new bike I got stopped by the police. Nothing happened," he said, but in looking back Bobby realizes that the police stopped him because he was riding through a predominantly white neighborhood and they must have been checking to be sure he had not stolen the bicycle.

Another Christmas Bobby's mother got him the 'Cadillac' of sleds, a Flexible Flyer. "Plane Street was the best sleigh riding place in town." What I liked very much about Bobby's stories is that he smiles and chuckles when he tells his stories.

He learned to swim at the basin at Grace Lord Park. As Bobby pointed out, "Let's get honest now. There are two deep holes in town. One Deep Hole was where the Falls come down and that was used by white folks. Then next to it there was the basin where black folks swan." I asked Bobby, "Did that bother you?"

He replied, "At the time? Not really. That's the way it was. Like going to the movies – we went upstairs and the white folks sat downstairs. That's the way it was." And that is what life was like in America for people of color during the 1940s and 1950s. Segregation was the rule rather than the exception.

Bobby loved baseball and was good enough to play as the catcher. "At that time Boonton was divided into sections – the Flats, Cabbage Hill, the Park and West End. Each part of town had baseball teams and we would play each other." (Lloyd recalls the West End part of town had a baseball team called the "Riverside Athletic Club.")

I asked Bobby if he participated in "mischief night," the night before Halloween when kids turned over trash cans, etc. His reply was simple. "On Plane Street everybody knew everybody. If you got out of hand, your mother or father didn't have to be there to chastise you and straighten you out. The neighbors did it! And when your parents came home then you got it again. That's the way it was."

Bobby remembered the fruit vendor. "Back in those days he would make the rounds through Boonton and unfortunately the last street he came to was our street."

Bobby enjoyed listening to the radio, and he especially liked to listen to the Joe Louis boxing fights. "You'd go out there and we'd be playing in the streets but when the fights came on the radio, we cleared out. Then, after the fight and Joe Louis had won, everybody would be back in the streets laughing with happiness."

With his mother and older sister Osie, Bobby attended services each week at the Bethel AME (African Methodist Episcopal) Church. "We went to Sunday school – Monday school – Tuesday school. And in those days, Sunday was Sunday! No movies. You dressed up. Everybody ate together around the table."

Bobby was approximately 14 years old when his mother sent him to boarding school at the New Jersey Manual Training and Industrial School in Bordentown, New Jersey. The school has been called the "Tuskegee of the North" after the renowned historically black Alabama University.

"I didn't like it at all," Bobbie said about his first months away. The school was co-ed and there were about 300 or 400 students. Half of the curriculum during the day was academics and the other half of the day we learned about carpentry, electricity, agriculture, etc." For that education, his mother paid $15 a month, and Bob worked part-time at school. This represented quite an expense to the family.

What eventually changed Bobby's mind about boarding school was his chance to sing in the choir, run on the track team, and to become a star half-back on the school's outstanding football team. I asked him if he was a half-back like my hero, Tiki Barber, who played for the New York Giants until a few years ago. Lloyd, who had been videotaping the interview, teased Bobby, "Chances are you weren't as good as Tiki!" Bobby shot back quickly, "I was even better. That was **my** sport!"

Bobby talked about his wife Margaret, recently deceased, whom he met at church, and he went on to brag about his children – Mark, Tracy, Cynthia, Bobbi and Roland. He said with awe, "I look at my kids – I've never had a bad day from one of them – not one!! You have to be blessed or somebody has to be guiding you."

From 1951 to 1955 Bob served in the Air Force. During this time, he trained in police work and spent two years in Japan as part of his military duty. One day, after he had been in Japan six months, he heard his name called. It was Alfonso Gilchrist of Boonton. He was the first person Bobby met who came from his hometown. "And so we got to talking back and forth and it gave me somebody to go with and so that was the first time I went off the military base into a town in Japan."

Bobby began as a Boonton policeman working the night shift (which was not easy as he and Margaret had their first two children just a year apart). "I was promoted to Sergeant 5 years later in 1962. I was promoted to Lieutenant 5 years later in 1967. Then 15 years later in 1985 I became Captain." In 1990, when the position came open due to the retirement of the former Chief, Bobby was recommended for the position of Police Chief and he served in that position until 1995.

Summing up his philosophy, Bobby said, "You should live right, treat people right and do the right thing. And it all eventually comes together." It sure has for Bobby Banks!

BEDNAR, BILL

BONANNI, DANNY

TREDWAY, BILL   Interview 10/15/09 – by Terry Charlton

Bill Bednar   **Danny Bonanni**   **Bill Tredway**

MEMORIES OF A BOONTON INTERVIEW

I felt like singing "Hail Hail the Gang's All Here!" about five minutes into my interview with these good friends and fellow Boontonites. This was not going to be the interview we originally planned on conducting. These friends came to our house to reminisce and that's exactly what they did. For over two hours we laughed as they shared memories together.

Let me introduce them.

1) Bill Bednar, whose career was as Boonton's Chief of Police,

2) Danny Bonanni was a Lieutenant in the Boonton police department,

3) Bill Tredway worked in his family's trucking business and

4) Lloyd Charlton whose career was as a test engineer for Picatinny.

They are men from the generation of people we all admire! Franklin D. Roosevelt said this was a 'generation of Americans who had a rendezvous with destiny.' How right he was.

1) All of them remember the Depression. "We had enough to eat and we learned to make due. We worked after school when we were growing up." Life was given to them – not on a silver platter - but with strings attached. They laughed and accepted the challenge.

2) Bill Bednar and Bill Tredway were drafted and served during World War II, and Lloyd served from 1945 to 1947 in Korea. Danny was in the Army and served for two years after the War. They felt the soldiers who served in WWII were the real heroes and Bill B, Danny and Bill T were ready to do their share. Being patriotic to them was not a duty. It was their privilege.

3) The word "accountability" is synonymous with these men. Combined: they have given more than 150 years of volunteerism to Boonton!! That number is probably much higher but in my short meeting with them I learned that

    a. Bill Bednar played with Harmony Drum Corps for years, as well as serving as Boonton's Police Chief,

    b. Danny Bonanni is a volunteer fireman today and has been in the Fire Department since1956, s well as a Police Lieutenant in the Boonton police, and

    c. Lloyd Charlton worked on the school board and, for over 50 years, has been a scout leader. As well as a Historical Society trustee and photographer for the Rockaway Valley Garden Club.

    d. But it is Bill Tredway who is hands down the most loyal volunteer with over 57 years as a firefighter and 20 years on the Kiwanis Ambulance squad.

With Lloyd, Bill T. and Bill B. having passed their 80th birthdays, they are coming to an age that includes aches and pains. Every day they read about the death of yet another friend. The world as they remember from years ago no longer exists.

So what do they do? They laugh and laugh and laugh some more!

And what do they laugh about? They tell the story about how the court needed an interpreter one day and their friend Tony Richards told the judge he knew Italian. When asked to inquire about the man's name, he went up to the man, spoke loudly, slowly and using broken English said, "What's a you name?" The judge burst out laughing.

They laugh at having to attend school - even in the dead of winter -wearing short pants until they reached the 4th grade when they could change to wearing three-quarter length pants called knickers.

They laugh about the times during the Depression that they tried to get coal from the train when it stopped at the Boonton train station to get water. (Coal was used to heat their homes.) Lloyd said his father remembered annoying the boatmen on the canal in the hopes the boatmen would throw coal at him and he could bring it home to his family.

They laugh about the first time they saw someone eat a banana sandwich for lunch.

Bill Bednar laughs about the time Harmony Drum Corps marched right into the Darress Theater to celebrate their victory after a parade. The moviegoers started shouting "Get them out of there" as the movie was at the most climatic moment.

Danny Bonanni laughs at the time when he was a young altar boy and was asked by the priest to take up the collection. Years ago people gave pennies, nickels and dimes so the basket got too heavy for him to lift and the people in the church started laughing.

Bill Tredway laughs about the time he was taking up the collection during a Mass at St. Patrick's Cathedral. He said to the other usher, "This collection basket is too small for such a large congregation." He was told, "Just keep shoving it down."

Another story was about the time Bill Bednar and his friends came out of the movie and climbed into Bill's car and turned it on. "Wow," said Bill, "That fire on Division Street must have been a big fire because I can still smell it in the car." Then they realized the car was on fire!

They all joked about the Diner in town they nicknamed the "Greasy Spoon." Once when someone came in and asked for the pound cake with the raisins on it, the owner said, "Here it is. It doesn't have raisins." And he waved away the flies.

They remember sad times, of course, because being in the police and fire departments, the tragedies in a small town was part of their daily lives. Bill Tredway remarked that over the years more than 10 people died while diving into the swimming basin called 'deep hole' in Grace Lord Park.

But whenever there was a lull in the conversation, someone would say, "Do you remember the guy who slept with his horses? He lived on Union Street and his name was Jake?" And off they'd go on another funny memory.

Bill Tredway bought along a list he compiled in 2004 of the stores on Main Street that he remembered from the 1930s and 1940s. After a cursory look, I counted 15 groceries, 2 diners (no restaurants), 4 department stores, lots of candy/ newspaper/ ice cream stores, 4 shoe repair shops, 6 bakeries and there was even a blacksmith shop on Washington Street.

They agree they were lucky to come of age in Boonton in a time when everybody helped each other and extended families lived nearby. Kids had lots of friends nearby to play with and that made every day filled with new adventures, good memories and laughter.

And after a solemn and reflective moment about the problems and heartaches of the Depression and World War II, one of them would say, "Hey, do you remember the time we used to drink the water out of the frozen pond because we told ourselves that because it was 'ice' that purified it?"

Never one to give up easily, Terry tried to use her interview questionnaire once again and said, "How did you learn about the attack on Pearl Harbor?"

Bill Bednar said, "I was watching the Panthers football game when Tony Belini walked up to me and solemnly said "We are at war!" And I replied "So what did I do to you?"

113

When Bill recognized his former scoutmaster in church last week, Bill made my husband Lloyd Charlton feel 10 feet tall. Their last meeting had been in the early 1950s! With a ready smile, Bill said he would be happy to be interviewed as "I grew up in a small town and lived in the same house throughout my childhood and there were many wonderful things about that."

"Our house had been a barn and my grandfather had it converted into a home for my Great Aunt Gladys Kingsley and she raised her family there." Lloyd remembered after high school he worked as a mailman in Boonton and complained that one time Bill's dog, a German Schnauser, nipped at his heels.

George Ross, Sr., Bill's grandfather, became President of a company called Huron Milling Company. After he retired Bill told us, "He devoted himself to trying to help other people and he gave many scholarships to kids from Boonton to go to college."

Bill recalled, "My grandfather was the first head of the Riverside Hospital (near Del's Village) and participated in the ground-breaking for the hospital." George Ross, Sr. started the Community Medical Group because there was no hospital in the area and Lloyd recalls that when he was a teenager he got his tonsils removed at the Community Medical Group.

Bill's father and uncle owned a car dealership in Dover, NJ and during WWII there were no cars for sale. "They went into the tire recapping business to survive," Bill recalls. His father was good at woodworking and Bill fondly remembers a beautiful dollhouse his dad made for his older sister Dagmar who recently died. "He made a barn for my brother and me. You could lift up one side of the barn and there were animals inside."

114

Bill's mother enjoyed playing "Canasta" with the family and one of her ingenious gifts was a zither that the family enjoyed playing.

Asked if Halloween's mischief night existed when he was growing up, Bill recalls, "Our neighbor Mr. Peterson taught us how to take a spool (from a spool of thread) and carve chunks out of the spool so it looked like a gear. He put it on a dowel and he rigged up a string, so that when you placed this up against somebody's window and you pulled on the string it would make a chattering on the window." Obviously, 'mischief night' was tamer in the 1950s than the 1930s and 1940s when young boys turned ash cans upside down or piled porch furniture against someone's front door.

Asked about childhood games he played with friends, Bill told us, "We played on the parking lot of the manse of the Presbyterian Church. The only drawback was that people used to walk their dogs there." He remembered going with the scouts, "We hiked up Tourne Park and did mirror signals down to somebody below."

As a young boy, Bill's appendix burst and he was extremely fortunate to have a doctor who administered penicillin (which was an experimental drug for the treatment of appendicitis at the time).

Here is another frightening experience Bill remembers. Lloyd's photos help describe the incident that happened in Grace Lord Park.

Lloyd said: "The Falls go into a basin with a big rock in the center of it. It narrows down to 3 ft. wide between huge rocks and then there is another basin which leads to the Arch Bridge."

Here is the story in Bill's own words:

"I was in my early teens and my two cousins, Peter and Charles, were also swimming in the pond just below Pond Bridge. And Charles wasn't up to swimming across the pond - he was a slower swimmer and a little guy and he got caught in the currents. So I tried to swim down to grab him to keep him from going over the Falls and he went over (and I am not sure if Peter went over or not) but I went over, too."

"I don't remember exactly, but the river gets narrow just below the Falls and I do remember going over the Falls and I do remember being underwater and I tumbled around upside down and I couldn't tell where was 'up.' It was dark and muddy so I closed my eyes and just said, 'I am going to float up' and that worked. And then I looked around for Charles and I couldn't see him. I panicked because the water was going fast down through the narrow part and down to the Arch Bridge and I thought, 'Charles is going through it.' I got out before I got to the Arch Bridge and I ran up and down the side of the river trying to find him. Fortunately, we found him and got him out. He was fine."

Lloyd said it succinctly when he said to Bill, "You and Charles were very lucky you both survived." In a recent interview with him Bill Tredway said, "Over the years more than 10 people died while diving into Deep Hole."

Bill said enthusiastically, "On the radio I loved listening to the Newark Country & Western station – Home Town Frolic." He especially enjoyed the children's programs that came on the radio between 5 and 6:30 p.m. daily, "Tom Mix, The Green Hornet, Jack Armstrong, the Cisco Kid and Bobby Benson and the B-Bar-B Riders."

In adolescence, Bill attended Morristown Beard, and then went to Princeton and Columbia for graduate school. The father of two children, Bill enjoyed his career in finance and the family lived in London for many years.

Asked about retirement, Bill said, "I feel less stress than at any time in my life." Remarried for the past 7 years, Bill and his wife Ginny enjoy their families and grandchildren, they travel frequently, and Bill's summer tan is a give-away that he enjoys playing golf. "We both feel very, very lucky for a lot of gifts that life has given to us."

Bill described his involvement with a school in Newark called "St. Philips Academy ... to give the children the same quality of education that kids have going to a really good public school."

His philosophy is "The biggest thing you can hope for in your children – is that they learn to love something. It doesn't matter what it is. It can be an animal – school -- anything – because once you do that it is possible for them to learn to love other things." It's easy to see that Bill's gratitude is what makes him a very nice person to know.

BOGUE, BOB AND LYNN -

Given only 45-minutes to conduct an interview with two fascinating people, I was immediately struck by how deeply they love each other. Lynn sat quietly next to Bob at the dining room table while he answered my questions. Now and then she would jump into the conversation and talk about Bob's artistic talents, his love and enjoyment of their children and his successful advertising career in New York.

I asked Bob how he met Lynn. He said they were stationed at Camp Pickett and Lynn was an Army motor pool driver. And? And? Bob looked at me and said, "I saw her and that was it!!!" At another point I asked Lynn if she was happy with settling down to live in Boonton Township. Lynn smiled a deep smile and responded, "I wanted to be wherever Bob was. That was home!!"

Bob interjected their home cost $5,500, that is, $35 a month!

On a biographical note, Lynn is so enthusiastic it's easy to see why Bob fell in love with her. She is trim and full of energy, and boasts of being adventurous as well as very athletic. She is a gracious hostess, bakes her own bread, adores her children, and remembers fondly joining the Women's Army Corps (WAC) during WW II. Lynn was a member of the North Carolina Polar Bear Club and only retired when she reached her 90th birthday.

On a biographical note, Bob Bogue was born in 1921. He recalled with fondness that in 1906 his dad was in the Navy and went around the world. The log his father kept is one of their most treasured family possessions. Bob was 8 years old when the market crashed and he distinctly remembers his parents talking about it. Then, in 1933, his father died of a heart attack at the age of 48. Bob was 12 when his mother got a job earning $15.00 per week at Jersey Central Power & Light and so they moved to Boonton so she could be close to her job. His neighbors on Schultz Street (now named West Main Street) were the Estlers and Lloyd Charlton.

After graduating from Boonton High School in 1939, Bob studied art in New York City at "CIS" – Commercial Illustration Studio – for two years and then worked in advertising in the City. He enlisted in the Army in World War II and while stationed at Camp Pickett, Virginia, he met Lynn, a member of the Women's Army Corps (WAC). They were immediately attracted to each other and were married in the Post Chapel. Part of Bob's military career was served in a hospital unit in England.

Bob returned to Boonton Township after the War where he purchased a house near the Rockaway River. He and Lynn raised their four children there – David, Scott, Leslie and Robin. Bob commuted to NYC to work in advertising and eventually co-owned a company called "Clement and Bogue." He retired in 1972 and they moved to North Carolina where they live today.

Having been a boy scout in Troop 1 in Boonton as a youth, Bob became a scout leader for about 20 years in the Township, including two years as Scoutmaster of Troup 69. He was a deacon in the Rockaway Valley Methodist Church and he and Oscar Kincaid built a stone wall that still stands between the Church and Valley Road, using stones they took from the fields of Oscar's farm.

In 2001, Lloyd Charlton commissioned Bob to paint a picture of Lloyd's home on Cornelia Street from photographs he sent to Bob. When the painting arrived at the house, Lloyd was so excited he sent Bob more old photos and postcards to work from and eventually Lloyd had received a dozen or more new painting of Boonton at the turn of the century done by Bob. In 2007, Lloyd was the curator for an exhibit of Bob Bogue's art in the Boonton Historical Society Museum and Boonton's Mayor Wekilsky awarded Bob a Town Proclamation for his work.

In January 2009, Lloyd Charlton published a book entitled *"The Artistry of Bob Bogue"* featuring 38 of Bob's paintings. This small book is available at Boonton's Historical Society gift shop and on "amazon.com."

Bob's best memories of his adolescence in Boonton revolve around riding his "Elgin bike" and playing sports with Whitfield Estler, his best friend and next door neighbor. "We played Rubber Ball and you didn't have to use a real bat. We used sticks! We played in the Estler yard." Sadly, yet another important person left Bob Bogue's life when Whitfield Estler died at age of 14 from complications resulting from a mastoid infection (see Don Estler's essay).

I said in the interview, "Don Estler told me a 'tall tale' and I want to know from you, Bob:

"Q: Do you remember Bull Estler?

BOB: Oh yeah. He was Don Estler's grandfather.

Q: Do you believe Bull Estler carried a piano all by himself?
BOB: Oh yeah. He carried our piano! I remember when we moved to a home in Boonton I saw Bull Estler put a tape around his head and around the piano and he carried it out to the truck."

Asked about the Depression, Bob told me he believes their house was 'marked' as a place to ask for food because his mother was always making sandwiches for the 'fellas' (hobos) who came to the door.

My next question was: "Bob, during World War II, did you ever worry that we might not win the War?"

Bob's reply was adamant and immediate! "We are invincible!!!! It never occurred to me."

I asked Bob, 'Is there something 'wonderful' about being a senior?" He laughed and replied with an emphatic "No!" Bob has arthritis and some hearing loss, but his sense of humor is certainly not slowing down.

Responding to my question, "What has given you joy in life?" Bob was quiet for a long moment and then responded with a catch in his voice, "I guess it was having a family. Our kids are such a big help to us!"

BOLCAR, STEPHEN -   Interview 03/19/10 – by Terry Charlton

Stephen and Emily Westura Bolcar greeted us at the door to their home on Boonton Avenue in March 2010. Steve is 92, of medium height and looks as energetic and trim as he did 70 years ago when he flew in 8 combat missions in a B24 during WWII. Steve was a gunner. His mind is so sharp he can still remember the names of his grammar school teachers.

He and Emily have been married 63 years and she is as 'quiet' as he is 'talkative.' Emily told me she does all the cooking, but when I asked her if she remembered any special radio programs she replied with her gentle smile, "Steve remembers that better." Steve interrupted the interview a half-dozen times to speak with loving concern to his wife. Emily, like the gracious hostess she is, insisted she wanted to stay next to Steve during our lengthy interview. (Sadly, Emily recently passed away a month or so ago.)

Steve pointed out that in their backyard, years and years ago, there was a chicken coop. Emily's next door neighbors were the Beiermeister family and Mae Beiermeister Wiswall (interview Feb. 9, 2010) was one of nine children. In the 1930s, Steve's mother-in-law, Mrs. Theresa Westura, would sell eggs to Mrs. Ora Beiermeister.

So meet 92 year old Stephen Bolcar - born in 1917 on Union Street, a lifelong Boonton resident. His ancestors came from Austria/ Hungary. "Why, did they immigrate to America?" I asked. Steve replied, "They all came here for one purpose - I don't care where they came from - they came for a better life."

In 1918, there was an epidemic of flu called the "Spanish flu" which killed 675,000 people in the United States alone. Steve remembers hearing that soldiers had to wear gauze masks during the epidemic.

The flu created an over-reaction of the immune system and the majority of those who died of the disease were young adults. Sadly, one of its victims was Stephen's mother. He recalled speaking to Evelyn Eckart's mother who shared a hospital room at Old Soul's Hospital (Morristown) with his mother. She told Steve, "Your mother called out, 'I want to see my baby' shortly before she died of the flu."

After his mother's tragic death, 15 month old Stephen came down with this same flu. His grandmother, grieving over the loss of his mother, rushed Stephen over to Dr. Carpenter's office. He told her, "Mrs. Bolcar, Stephen will live only 2 weeks." And she replied vehemently, "Oh no, he will not die!" Using a home remedy purgative, she brought Stephen back to health. Three months later Dr. Carpenter died.

Steve's dad worked in a silk mill on Monroe Street (the building that today has a car on the roof). "His salary was $.50 cents a day, or $5.00 every two weeks." Steve spoke lovingly about his grandparents who brought him up.

When Stephen was a teenager his grandfather came to him and said, "Steve, I don't want you to go back to school. We need the money." Despite good grades and begging for a chance to stay in school, Stephen put his disappointment aside and did what Stephen does best -- he was dutiful in helping his family. In fact, it is apparent Stephen Bolcar has always been and always will be dutiful. His integrity would never be questioned because as Stephen says, "I could never lie to you. I'd only be lying to myself."

His first job was working for the WPA (Works Progress Admin.), which was a government-run public works program that gave jobs to the unemployed during the Depression. Stephen brags, "My first job was at the astronomical salary of $48 a month."

As he neared adulthood, Steve was at a dance at Sokol Hall. Calling up all his courage, as the dance was coming to an end he went up to a young girl and said, "Ms. Emily Westura, May I have this dance with you?" She replied jokingly, "I don't dance with kids."

Shortly after that, this time it was Emily who had to do the asking! "Stephen," she said timidly, "May I have this dance?" To which Stephen replied, "I'll have to ask my father and mother."

So started a romance that has lasted a lifetime. Emily and Stephen brag about their three wonderful children Judy, Bruce and Alan. Seeing a photo of Emily taken around 1946, Emily was a gorgeous teenager and, as Steve pointed out, her inner beauty continues to shine through 63 years of marriage.

So what it is like to:

1) Survive an epidemic in 1918?

2) Work during your adolescence for the WPA?

3) Serve in the Air Force during WWII -- fly on 8 missions -- and also survive a plane crash?

Steve was stationed in Tibenhem, England 100 miles north of London and 13 miles southwest west of Norwich from September 1944 to May 1945. Stephen flew eight missions in a B24 as a gunner. He remembers they had to fly into the sunshine and wore special sunglasses to cut down the glare. As Steve pointed out, "It was a definite disadvantage because the German Air Force would fly at us with their backs to the sun."

On September 27, 1944 when Steve had just arrived in Tibenhem, he learned that thirty-nine B-24's left Tibenhem for Kassell, Germany and only 12 aircraft came back. It was a terrible loss.

On October 18, 1944 Steve's pilot was selected to fly one of three B24s going to Green Castle, Ireland. Steve was not chosen for that flight. Steve related this story: "Two B-24s were scrapped for usable parts and 24 men were returning in one of the B24s. It started to have mechanical failure and the plane exploded and all 24 men lost their lives at Landican, England."

The French Croix de Guerre (it's one of France's highest honors) was awarded – not individually – but to the 445th Bomb Group. "We had the most devastating losses of the 8th Air Force Squadron."

On February 24, 1945 Sergeant Stephen Bolcar, a member of the 445th Bombardment Squadron, was on a mission when the aircraft ran into trouble. Shortly after takeoff, Steve (working as a gunner) reported to the pilot that engine #1 started to spew fire and then began to blaze. The pilot shut down the engine immediately and decided to return to the airfield, but at the last minute was instructed not to land because of the 20 napalm bombs on board.

As the plane flew low enough to touch treetops while trying to gain altitude unsuccessfully, Steve remembered, "I blessed myself and said, 'God, make it quick or bring me through' -- which He did."

And then "We hit." And in Steve's exact words ...

- "Now – the first time I tried to get up ... the black smoke hit me in the face and I went down.
- I tried once more.
- Finally, I said, "You jerk. Hold your breath for a second like you were swimming." And I did. And I got up." Ground crew had a problem with the windows, so the aircraft left without them.
- "And the fella from Detroit Michigan – George Van Landenham – he was a 6 ft. tall and I had to push him out the window." Steve was able to escape through the window opening.
- "And we got out. And when you see the crash pictures you'll see – from the two twin tail sections – the aircraft was cut in half. That was all that was left."

Steve suffered first degree burns on the right side of his face but miraculously he recovered the vision in his right eye. He suffered multiple cuts on his body, as well.

Of the 10 men on board, five men were killed and five men survived.

"I came back to the United States in May 1945 and landed at what was then named 'Windsor Army Air Base' in Windsor CT. I came out of the airplane and I kissed the concrete. Then I found out someone stole all my clothing."

I am proud to have interviewed such a distinguished American soldier who faced the enemy courageously and who had a very close call with death! Perhaps in another interview we can elaborate about Steve's "Boonton memories" but for today - this is the story I am proud to retell.

When Steve returned from the War, Steve followed the old Slovak custom of going to Emily's parents first to ask for Emily's hand in marriage. When they agreed, he went to Emily and asked her to marry him. She replied affirmatively and then added, "I thought you were taking your time!!"

CARMAN, MARY (LEVA) -   Interview 02/05/10 – by Terry Charlton

Mary Carman maintains her own home, lives independently and loves to watch game shows on television. Of medium height, Mary is sharp as a tack! She is slim, well dressed and a gracious hostess when we visited her home for this interview. When I mentioned that she would be turning 90, Mary was quick to point out that she already had turned 90 and was, in fact, "90 and 1/2 years old." Pointing to a posterboard of photos given to her at her 90th birthday party at the Elks Club, Mary said she displays the photos in her living room because seeing them every day gives her great pleasure.

Since the focus of our interview is life in the early part of this century, Mary was a perfect person to interview. Asked about siblings, Mary said she was the first and then there was Gloria, Joe and then Jim. Mary's voice took on a somber note when she told us how much her mother had suffered when her two year old baby sister, Carmella, died after a severe laryngitis infection.

The firstborn child in an immigrant family, Mary started working at the pocketbook factory after completing 9th grade because, as she said, "At that time you had to go to work for the family." Her parents came from Italy and her father worked as a landscaper.

Mary remembers when her brother Joe (who was 7 years younger than she) insisted he had to listen to "The Lone Ranger" on the radio. "My sister and Gloria and I had to listen to it, too."

But that's typical of Mary Carman. She focuses on everyone but herself. In fact, she remembers that when the black people were required to go to the back of the bus, she and her husband Nate always "sat in the back of the bus, too." Her spirit is very generous, "If someone needs help I like to help them."

Asked about an early childhood memory, Mary – who was born in 1919 - remembers "We had to run out of our houses because they said they were going to bomb you. We lived on Old Boonton Road – and all of us got together on the sidewalk. I was very little then but thank God nothing happened. It was just a rumor."

Mary recalls that during the Depression, when hobos would knock on the door looking for a handout, "Everybody was nice! We'd have a picnic table in the back yard and mother would make them a sandwich and give them a drink."

I believe Mary had a wonderful role model in her mother! As Mary said, "My mother was like a 'pal' with me – a real friend and a good mother!" When Nate asked Mary for a date on a Sunday (a day dedicated to family visiting) Mary asked permission and her mother said "'Ok, go ahead.' And that's how I started dating Nate."

"Mother was really modern. We were proud of her."

"Mother was a good money saver. We took the bus over to Paterson (to go clothing shopping) and she'd say to the storekeeper, 'Can you lower the price?' and they always would!"

"We had an old Dodge and Alex (Scerbo) taught mother how to drive."

"My mother loved the water and we used to go to the seashore at Long Branch."

"Mother went to night school; she was a real trooper."

In fact, it was her mother's swift action that might have even saved Mary's life. "One day my mother took me out of the crib and put me down. I think I was about 4-1/2 and then I wouldn't stand up. I kept falling down. And she thought I was playing with her. She said, "Come on now. I've got a lot to do today." Then I started crying. So then she knew something was wrong. She took me over to Mrs. Sauchelli (Anna's mother). She was – they used to say – like a 'witch.' She took me and put me in water and massaged me right away and then my mother took me to Dr. Taylor and he said I had POLIO and he operated – I have a scar down my leg."

126

Polio continued to be a very real threat to children throughout the 1940s, even after penicillin came into use in the 1930s. To this day, polio still does not have a cure. However, in the 1950s the Salk vaccine was developed that prevented polio and this disease has just about been eradicated.

Asked about school memories, Mary said, "I liked all the teachers. They were all nice. There was one who pulled on her shoulder strap all the time." Lloyd said, "Oh that was Mrs. Leonard!" Such a small gesture but it made a lifelong impression! She told me that Gilda Micconi sold tickets at the State Theater and that the manager was called Dutchy because he was Dutch.

Mary's brother Jimmy died of a heart attack several years ago. Lloyd remarked, "Jimmy worked all the way up from a lineman at Jersey Central Power Company to the CEO of the Company!" Mary's remembered that, "Jimmy didn't act like a showoff. He was down to earth. He was so nice."

Nate Carman was the love of her life. He worked as a foreman at E.F. Drew. "He was a loving man." Father Murphy married them in 1945 at Our Lady of Mt. Carmel Catholic Church; they honeymooned for three days in NYC and spent $5,000 to buy the house she is currently living in on Intervale Road.

Nate was a volunteer fireman in Parsippany and Mary is still an auxiliary member of the fire department. "We used to go up to the cars driving by and ask for donations of money."

Nate and Mary have three wonderful children, Dan, Diane and Mary, and seven amazing grandchildren – all of whom are -- you guessed it! "They are SO NICE!"

What gives Mary the most joy? It's simple. Mary loves family gatherings! And she's already picked out what to wear to her brother Joe's birthday party on February 11th.

CASCELLA, ERNESTINE (PREVOST) -Interview 12/17/09 – by Terry Charlton

On meeting Ernestine Prevost Cascella, I was struck by how pretty she is. She studied to be a model after graduating high school but she wasn't tall enough at only 5 feet 6 inches. Instead, Ernestine climbed the corporate ladder and became a buyer at Quackenbush (later Sterns) Department Store. At the store's regular fashion shows Ernestine had fun modeling the spring line.

"Ernie" (her nickname) lives with her husband on Birch Street, the home she has lived in for her entire life. Every room on the first floor is spacious and sun-filled and connected to the other rooms by pocket doors. And because of Ernestine's impeccable style in decorating, my head was swiveling non-stop. When she and Tom Cascella decided to marry in the 1960s, she remembers that she had to get permission at work to take the day off to get married because it was a "Sale Day."

Ernestine is a member of the "Catholic Daughters" at Mt. Carmel Church raising money for charity. She is on the Mt. Carmel Alumni Committee raising money for the grammar school. She is on Boonton High School Class of 1944 Reunion Committee getting classmates together. And, more importantly, Ernie is visiting shut-in friends and bringing them her happy disposition, support, help and comfort.

Her grandparents came from Italy and Ernie remembers when her grandfather died. She was seven years old and recalls that they put a big wreath on the front door and her grandfather was laid out in the parlor. Death, life, work – she was taught that was all part of life's experiences. Grandma took over the housekeeping when Ernie's mother went to work at the Van Raalte, a business that made hosiery, undergarments and lingerie and was located on Myrtle Street.

"Monday was wash day -Tuesday – Wednesday – every day had routines because there was so much to do before washing machines," Ernie recalls.

Her dad ran a taxi service in town and also worked as a short order cook at the diner where Plane Street meets Main Street. The building was an old railroad car and she remembers that you entered at the end of the diner by sliding the door sideways. She doesn't remember booths or tables in the diner – just rows of stools at the counter.

Attending Mt. Carmel Catholic grammar school wearing her red tie, white middy blouse and navy blue skirt, Ernestine enjoyed school. She liked taking tap dancing lessons from Mr. Downey at the building that was used by the Masons but is now called the Knights of Columbus.

The joy of her adolescence was attending Boonton High School, making new friends and participating in the high school "Fashion Club." In school she loved playing basketball, enjoyed the archery classes and loved the noon dances in the gym. She and her friends would go up by the Powerville Dam where they rented canoes at Decker's and they would paddle up the river.

The highlight of the week was the Friday night dances at the Cross Club (the old school building on the Mt. Carmel property). "We had ping pong, shuffleboard, a library. You could play basketball upstairs. There was never trouble. Father Murphy was good with the youth and he gave us some place to go all the time."

A family story going back to a time when she was very young, recalls that Ernie got a high fever. Grandma Provost came up with a remedy of packing onions around both of her wrists and that broke the fever. She remembers the family using mustard plasters on her chest but that was definitely not one of her favorite cures.

A family friend, Dr. Muzetto, was telling Ernie's grandmother that his wife was sick. Her grandmother immediately said, "Ernestine (then about 8) will come down and help you." As Ernie put it, "Here I am this little girl going down to clean Dr Muzetto's house – which I didn't know too much about. I can remember they gave me 25 cents and I sat down and ate macaroni for dinner with them."

Family activity centered around a giant jigsaw puzzle always on the dining room table and listening to their favorite radio shows like Major Bows Original Amateur Hour or Bishop Sheen's 30-minute radio program every week.

Ernie had her own pair of white ice skates and loved to go skating at Hillary's Pond. She remembers it was often very crowded and you had to be careful of the tree stumps coming up through the ice. Lloyd Charlton said that Hillary's Pond was not a natural lake. They had cut down the trees, but left the stumps, dammed it up and then flooded it. So that was why there were stumps around the edges of the pond coming through the ice.

Ernie believes that her father had to be about 40 when he was drafted during World War II. He was in the Navy on the Ticonderoga Aircraft Carrier that served in several campaigns in the Pacific and earned 5 battle stars. But her father's favorite memory was the time the ship was sailing along calmly and then suddenly changed course sending all the crew running upstairs to their battle stations and sending all the eggs flying off the kitchen counter.

Asked who influenced her life, Ernestine said "My mother. She was a very nice lady. She always promoted us children. I could have gone to Caldwell College if I wanted to."

With a network of extended family surrounding her, Ernie grew up with lots of love and a house full of hard working people to emulate who cared for each other as well as contributed to those less fortunate in the community.

CHARLTON - ROBERT AND BARBARA (MABEY) -Interview 12/07/09 –
by Terry Charlton

Robert Charlton would not win first prize in a spirited debate because he is a quiet, unassuming man, but he would win first prize for congeniality. Born in 1921, Robert grew up in Boonton during the Depression. Robert spent three years in the Air Force stationed in the United States as a mechanic working on A20s, B25s and B56s during World War II. I asked Robert if people worried that America might not win World War II and he replied, "Sometimes it seemed pretty bleak from news reports but – we figured – we'll make out all right!"

Besides being easygoing, Robert is also honest, loyal and very laid-back. He raised two beautiful daughters, Mitzi and Rhea, and after 44 years of marriage, he suffered the loss of his wife Bell to cancer.

Fate changed the course of his life when Robert met and fell in love with Barbara Mabey (also widowed), to whom he has been married for the last 20 years. They live in Towaco. I asked Robert if he was born 'at home' (rather than in a hospital) and his wife Barbara quipped, "He was born in a stable!" She is the Charlie McCarthy to his Edgar Bergen and it makes their marriage work very well.

In actuality, Robert was born in the building that is now the Jim Carroll insurance agency. He was surrounded by other "Charlton relatives," witness his four uncles and at least eight cousins. Robert's dad worked in the Charlton family business delivering coal and ice. His Mom, Lillian, worked in a clothing store called Kottler and Goodman, which was located where Venturini's Deli is today.

Robert remembers playing Kick the Can, Red Light and Tag, as well as checkers, dominos and cards. He loved sports but admitted he wasn't much good at them when he played at the West Boonton Ball Field (now Riverside Hospital). His favorite gift was a bike. He often went swimming at the end of Chestnut Street. He enjoyed radio shows like "Jack Armstrong," "Bobby Benson," and"The First Nighter" program which was a long-running radio comedy-drama series broadcast from 1930 to 1953.

He remembers having mumps, measles and chicken pox "one after the other." From where he lived near Del's Village, Robert walked a mile and a quarter to Boonton High School. As he recalls, "It didn't matter whether it snowed or rained or haled or it was sunshine. You went to school every day."

Asked if he had any special memories of growing up, he said, "I liked it when the Firemen's Parade came to the ball park where Riverside Hospital is today. When the men were setting up the rides they would put us kids on the merry-go-round, ferris wheel and the swings for an hour while they were adjusting them. Then after the Fair closed each night we would go around to the various booths looking for change that people dropped. I used to make a couple of bucks a day that way!"

Asked about the Depression, Robert said, "Everyone was poor. What could you do? You had to live with it." In fact, the thing he most remembered was wearing the same clothes for several years. He laughed as he told me, "The clothes would start with sleeves way too long and in the last year the shirts sleeves were way too short."

An avid camper who has driven his trailer across America and through parts of Canada, Robert misses the fact that he can't do all the things he used to do. But when asked "What is the best part of being a senior citizen?" he chuckled, "I think to myself, I am so glad I don't have to drive to work in so much traffic like they have to do today."

That's Robert's personality in a nutshell. A nice guy who doesn't sweat the small stuff and, come to think of it, everything is small stuff!

CONDON, AL AND GRACE (FANNING) -Interview 07/27/10 –

by Terry Charlton

We sit visiting in the living room looking out of a picture window to a garden with its vibrantly colorful flowers. The birds and butterflies seem to be enjoying the garden, too. Al talks about baking cookies and mailing them to their children. Grace tells us she delights in curling up with a book about American history, or working on a jigsaw puzzle, especially if it features birds.

Grace Condon is so gracious, she makes you smile. Contrary to some marriages where put-down humor, veiled sarcasm, or "I told you so" mentality is evident, Grace loves Al and it shows. No – she adores Al!

Al's conversation is so enthusiastic he could be a game show host. He has a 'joy for life' that lights up his face as he talks with delight about his numerous projects. Al and Grace sit close together on the couch whispering to each other ...

"Tell them the story about your sunburn,"
"Tell them about your spinning wheel."

It is remarkable that 59 years of marriage has only multiplied their happiness at being in each other's company.

My husband Lloyd Charlton and Al Condon have gone through school together and it was Al who introduced Lloyd to scouting. In that era, people didn't talk about sadness and it was not polite to ask questions so Al never talked about growing up without his father in residence. Instead, Al regaled us with stories of Bobo and Chubby – the dogs he and his brother Tom had for a short time.

133

Asked about part-time employment growing up, Grace mentioned that she worked in the school's Guidance Office during school hours in exchange for which she didn't have to take the 6th marking period year-end tests. Aside from picking strawberries for a few weeks, Grace didn't work during high school. Al, on the other hand, had lots of jobs -- delivery boy, shoveling snow, kitchen help at a camp, camp counselor, and his favorite job – working in Harry's Bakery, where he reported for work at 6 p.m. on Friday and left at 6 a.m. the next morning.

Grace had lots of happy memories about birthdays, Christmas celebrations and wearing home-made Halloween costumes. Al had happy memories about camping out with the scouts and working to achieve the 21 merit badge requirements necessary to earn the highest honor awarded, becoming an Eagle Scout. Both remember going to the Elks Club for a Christmas party where Santa came and handed out Christmas stockings to the less fortunate children in town.

Asked about vendors, "I remember the banana man" said Grace. "The ice man brought a big piece of ice for our icebox and only charged 10 cents." She remembers a man who came by in a truck ringing some jungle bells and yelling, "Rags. We buy Rags." Paper was valuable at that time and you could bring paper to Mr. Basch. He would weigh the papers and pay you a few cents for them. With 'penny candy' a staple of all candy stores, if you found an empty soda bottle and brought it back to the store you'd get a 2 cent deposit – just enough for some delicious candy dots.

Not one to brag, it took some coaxing to get Grace to say she was "good" at jump rope at school recess. She also remembers playing "Russia" where you threw a ball against a building while performing feats like clapping your hands behind your back and – admittedly – she was good at that, too. She loved to go roller skating with her friend Marion. Each of them would wear one skate which was held on their shoe with a piece of elastic. "We would pump with one foot – just like you do on a skooter." They liked to go over to the church playground where the ground had smooth black slates just perfect for skating.

I forgot to mention something about Al. His quick repartee makes talking to him quite a lot of fun. At one point when Lloyd described how, during the Depression, hobos would sometimes come to his house for a sandwich, Al was quick to say, "Hey! That was me!!!!"

When he graduated high school, Al joined the Air Corps but soon learned he was color blind and could not go into flying. Brother Jack flew 25 – possibly 35 missions during WWII. Brother Tom received two Purple Hearts while serving in the 10th Mountain Division. "But," Al reflected with quietness, "they never talked about it."

134

During his two years in the military, "I learned Morse Code as a radio operator and was sent to the Azore Islands (off the coast of Portugal) and I would contact the airplanes by code and get them close enough to the airport to be brought in by 'voice' operators."

For his working career, Al worked as a tool maker, a job he held for 33 years until the company sold the business. When she graduated high school, Grace worked for 3-1/2 years as a secretary at Dixon Bros.

Coming back to Boonton after the War, a friend told Al about Grace – and he called her up. I should have known better than to ask why he liked Grace. With his sharp wit, he quickly replied, "She was single."

Within less than a year Al and Grace were married and soon became quite busy raising their large family which included making room in their home for Grace's parents to move in. It's charming to hear Al and Grace speak with justifiable pride about their children and grandchildren. They are especially proud that their children are such good people, who are not only successful but well educated.

As the interview came to an end, I asked Al if having such a large family worried him, and he replied, "I never thought about it. Whatever came along in life was fine."

I asked Grace if she enjoyed any of our modern inventions like computer and cell phones. She laughingly replied that she wondered why people felt that they had to talk on cell phones while in places like the grocery store or in the doctor's office.

"Al," I said, "What is the best part of your daily life? Do you like your morning coffee or to take a long walk?"

His response was so immediate and so heartfelt it took my breath away.

"HER!" Al said with enthusiam. "GRACE IS THE JOY OF MY LIFE."

Grace responded in her soft voice, "That was the nicest thing to say."

"We have been so fortunate," they repeated over and over during the one-hour interview.

And Grace, in recalling their 59 years together, ended our interview exclaiming with great pleasure: **"And we'd do it all again!"**

DI EDUARDO, MARIE -

Interview 04/07/10 – by Terry Charlton

When I first met Marie at one of the Historical Society functions, she was working at the cash register as a volunteer. I liked her at once because – how many 90 year old folks do you meet who can talk about vacations to Peru, Argentina, Brazil, Chile, Kenya, most of the countries of Europe, India, China, Japan, Egypt, Australia, New Zealand, Hawaii and Alaska – to name just some of her trips! I knew Marie would give us a fascinating interview story.

To say "Little Marie" is 4' 10" is a gross exaggeration! At 93 she still lives independently in a house built in the 1860s for which she paid $2,200 in 1940. Marie told us her childhood was spent on a farm in Keyport, NJ and her memories of her early life were sad. "My mother gave birth to a little boy and they got peritonitis and died. Other personal tragedies included losing a brother and a sister during her childhood. Marie recalls that eventually her father remarried and her stepmother wasn't very loving.

"At that time the farm was like a little village with buildings on it. We had horses, cows, pigs, chickens and lots of farm equipment." Marie recalls that her stepmother did the cooking but "when I came home from school I had to wash the lunch dishes and later the evening dishes." Then she would start her farming chores. "I don't remember half the stuff that happened because it was no fun! I did get a half-day off on Sunday!"

It was a childhood without parties, friends visiting and family adventures. I asked her about her favorite toy and she replied humorously, "You mean the rake or the hoe?" Kids didn't get toys then. "Growing up we had 2 outfits. You'd wear the same outfit for a week, wash it and put it on again. There were no closets in those days!" In fact she remembers Christmas was special because she got walnuts and an orange.

Fast forward a dozen years and Marie met, married and had four children with the nicest guy in Boonton, Nano Di Eduardo. They moved into a house on Grant Street but then decided to move to the farm after her dad had a heart attack and died. Tragedy befell this young family when her husband was killed in a farm accident leaving Marie alone to bring up their four children who were then only 5, 4, 3 and 1. And she did. "It was hard! There was no such thing as insurance back in those days!"

Marie worked for 25 years at Boonton Handbag doing piece-work. Remembering Mr. Patarnik, the owner, she said, "You couldn't find a nicer person than him." Her fondest memories of Boonton included seeing the kids march in the Labor Day Parades as Boy Scouts and girl scouts and swimming in the Rockaway River down on Monroe Street. With wonderful neighbors who also had large families, her kids always had friends to play with, movie money that was easy to earn and lots of birthday and graduation parties!

It felt a little silly to ask Marie if she ever worked as a volunteer since her life was so full of achievements. But I knew she is still volunteering at the Historical Society so I asked, "Did you ever volunteer?" To my amazement, she said, "Of course. I would walk up to the Riverside Hospital and work at the front desk. (Round trip that would be at least several miles!) I put in 5,000 hours as a volunteer before the Hospital closed."

Marie is a role model! She is not only charitable and big-hearted, but her spirit is indomitible.

Tragically, Marie suffered the worst punishment a parent can endure when her oldest son Joseph died of complications of a wound he received while serving in Vietnam. His military service medals include the Medal of Honor and they are displayed proudly on a bookcase in her living room. It was only when she was talking about her son Joseph that I think Marie was fighting back tears.

Since she is so lively, humorous, kind-hearted and friendly, I had to ask, "Marie, how did you do it? Where do you find the courage when life goes from tough to almost impossible?"

She replied simply, "You get through it because you have no choice. And _HE_ helps upstairs, too."

Despite so many years of work, when asked about her enjoyment of retirement, Marie countered, "I'd rather be working!" Her energy is amazing!

"What advice would you want to give to the next generation?" I anticipated she would say, "Get up and keep fighting!"

Instead, she replied emphatically, "'***Enjoy Life!!***!" With all her many exotic trips, Marie turned her senior years into her golden years!!!   Marie enjoys her children, grandchildren, friends, gardening, crosswords, travel – "I don't have time to get lonesome."

Marie looked back on her life and said, "I am thankful!" It's really neat to have a friend who can think that way!

DUNN, JULIA –

At 94, Julia Dunn is still known for wearing stylish clothes (sadly, just a few months ago Julia passed away). She is a trim size 6, too! And Julia is nothing if not charming!

* Julia lives in the house where she was born 94 years ago

* Julia retired in 1998 from Dr. Moya-Mendez' office after working in that same office for 70 years

* Julia is a member of the "Catholic Daughters" at Mt. Carmel Catholic Church and has been active for over 70 years doing charity work

* Julia admits she absolutely loves to eat cake

* Julia's greatest joy is attending Mt. Carmel for church services

Julia is a charming older Boontonite. She is easygoing and I found myself smiling when I talked to her. As she told me, she has 'gotten over' a bout of cancer, a broken arm and a broken hip so her health is very good. She lives in her home in which she was born. She has a wonderful caregiver and she told me she feels "joy" whenever a neighbor drops by.

Julia loved her work as secretary to Dr. Riscom, Dr. Rickert and then Dr. Moya-Mendez in a career that spanned over seven decades. Each doctor occupied the same space in the Pilgrim Apartments building at Birch and Church Streets, one block from Julia's house. She started as a secretary, learned how to do bookkeeping, maintained patient records accurately and made doctor appointments for thousands of people.

As a child, Julia describes herself as a quiet child who liked to read, to listen to classical music and to play games with her friends. Her favorite toy was a doll. Three of her sisters became Dominican nuns, and when I asked Julia why she didn't follow in their footsteps, she replied, "Nobody asked me!"

Julia's sister Helen wrote the Boonton High School song and was a good writer who wrote about Boonton of long ago. Julia's hobby was to do any type of needlepoint and she can still knit and crochet today. Plus, Julia loved to do the baking for all family events.

Julia's Dad was in the Harmony Fire Department for 50 years, and her brother Jack was Boonton's Chief of Police. Julia joined the Catholic Daughters (a charitable group associated with Mt. Carmel Church) and contributed to the Indians in South Dakota. In fact Julia actually made six trips by herself to visit the Indians over the years delivering boxes of blankets, and knitted and crocheted products made by the ladies of the Catholic Daughters.

I asked Julia what she liked best about retirement. And she replied quickly, "I'd rather work."

"Julia," I asked as my final question, "Is there anything hard about being a senior?" She replied with a quick smile, "No. People are very kind to me." Maybe it's because she is the nicest person in Boonton. I felt it was a privilege just to be in her presence and it was a joy to get the chance to interview her.

DURRER, MARGOT (AMMANN) -   Interview 01/29/10 – by Terry Charlton

Dr. Margot Durrer is a very easygoing person who seems to see life through a prism of laughter. She's trim and petite and enjoys swimming at a pool near her apartment on the Upper East Side in NYC.

At the graduation ceremony from Boonton High School, Class of 1939, Gay Crosby was the valedictorian and, as Class President, Margot preceded her with a farewell speech. It began to rain just as Margot finished her speech and the ceremony had to be hurriedly moved indoors. She attended Vassar and then pursued a medical degree at New York Medical College. She specialized in obstetrics and gynecology and opened her practice on 81st and Park. In 1960 she wed Dr. Gustav Durrer, a dentist practicing in New York City, and they had 41 happy years of marriage before he died in 2001. She hinted, "As doctors, we practiced at opposite ends."

Dr. Durrer grew up as Margot Ammann, youngest child of Othmar Ammann, a Swiss-born civil engineer specializing in long span bridges. They lived on "Rockaway Avenue" (now called "Rockaway Street"). Othmar Ammann was responsible for designing six major bridges around Manhattan including the Bayonne Bridge, the George Washington Bridge and the Verrazano-Narrows Bridge. The George Washington Bridge was his first. Its span length was two times longer than any existing bridge at that time. "I always called the bridge my older sister." Said Margot, "… I was a little bit in competition with this bridge!"

In 2005 Boonton's *Othmar Ammann Bridge* was completed and opened for traffic. It is located at the end of Washington Street where it crosses the Rockaway River.

July 2005 ceremony for the opening of Boonton's *Othmar Ammann Bridge*.

141

Dr. Durrer is shown here standing in front of the Bridge's dedication plaque.

Othmar Ammann came to New York from Switzerland as a young man with the intention to stay a year, but found his lifework in building bridges in and around New York City, as well as working as a consultant on the Golden Gate Bridge.

When she was born in 1922, Margot's brothers Werner and Andy were 12 and 15 years older, respectively. She remembers that, in lieu of playing with dolls, she preferred to go with the neighborhood boys who used to shoot and skin squirrels. During her childhood, Margot traveled several times to Switzerland with her parents. She learned to speak the Swiss dialect and to appreciate her Swiss heritage.

She hated the "fire and brimstone" weekly lectures given by the Director at St. John's School (now Wilson School) where she attended until the 3rd grade. She was then transferred to the Harrison Street School. She walked through the woods to get to school each day. At the southern end she passed by the old turntable tracks of the railroad. An old pottery kiln was still standing there, with a cable protruding from the back. "Someone told me there was a lion in the kiln so it was a bit scary to walk past it."

Margot recalls that her cocker spaniel always howled when the fire siren went off every day at noon. She also remembered that in the evening after a hot summer day before the existence of television, air conditioning and the computer, the children would run under the sprinklers, play games or chase fireflies, while the adults would relax and visit with neighbors out on their front porches.

While the George Washington Bridge was under construction in 1927, "Every Sunday father and I would walk to the Tourne and climb to the top of the tower. From there, father could see the progress on the construction of the New Jersey tower of the 'Hudson River Bridge' which was later renamed the 'George Washington Bridge.' But the best part was that on the way back we would stop at the Kozy Korner and have an ice cream."

When enough town folk complained about overturned trash cans and trampled gardens, the first Boonton Halloween Parade was organized. Margot and her friend Amy enjoyed being "Mickey" and "Minnie" in that first parade!

"Fun was not the object of growing up" she was told. She felt her parents "Blessed me with a feeling of obligation to society ... to learn to share ... and just do your best." The lesson she learned was to prepare for success so that, as evidenced by her father's career, "When the door of opportunity opened you walked through it."

"You can't forget coming in under the stage," Margot recalls when asked if she remembered the State Theater. Election Day stands out in her mind. "First of all, father stayed home from work that day. Mother put on her best suit. And neighbors met at the gas station by the foot of Essex Avenue to vote. In the evening we went to the movies at the State Theater. A pianist played music during the intermission and we listened to the election results."

When she was attending medical school in New York City she commuted each day and, with the War time "double daylight savings," she would have to get up and leave the house at 7 a.m. – which was in reality 5 a.m. She remembers seeing the moon when she was walking to the station in the winter and it was "very cold!"

In 1935, two years after her mother died of breast cancer, her father remarried and her new step-mother brought along Edna, a young Swiss girl who had worked for her in California. Edna was 5 years older than Margot. Her extensive cartoon drawings depicting "Family Events from 1935-1950" are Margot's most cherished treasures today.

During WWII gas, oil, sugar and other essentials were rationed. Edna's drawings capture those memories with much humor. Margot said, "Here's her drawing of the oil man and it shows him sitting in the best chair in the living room smoking a cigar. Even our cocker spaniel is sitting up in front of him begging for more heating oil." Another cartoon is of Edna bringing in some tea on a tray and saying to the guest, "How much sugar do you want – One lump? Or none?"

Edna volunteered to be a block captain. In another drawing she hears the "blackout whistle" and literally drops the family dinner on the kitchen floor as she is dashing out of the house to assume her duties.

Margot remembers that some of her teachers took time to help her and several other students prepare for the college entrance boards. "This gave us a feeling of responsibility and a sense of gratitude to be able to attend college."

Asked what is difficult about being a senior citizen, Margot complains that "short term memory loss is no fun." Dealing with this and other 'inconveniences' requires a good sense of humor.

Asked what is best about being a senior citizen, Margot told us a story about trying to replace a broken neon light bulb and being told, "I'm sorry, lady, the bulb is obsolete." And I thought, "Why it's only 40 years old!!!!" But suddenly, it dawned on Margot that she, too, is "obsolete." This idea gave her a sudden delighted independence from obligations. "I am also irreplaceable!" From now on, it's all fun and games!"

ESTLER, DON & CHARLTON, LLOYD -Interview 12/08/09 by Terry Charlton

Don Estler   Lloyd Charlton

Don and Lloyd are lifelong friends. Both men were born in 1927. They went to the same school and lived across the street from one another. Both men are still very trim and fit and both men can talk for hours about growing up in Boonton! I anticipated they would talk for 45 minutes (i.e., 2,500 words), but they stopped talking only because the videotape ran out (at 9,800 words). My interview questions were never completed because we ran out of time.

The reason? Well I opened the conversation by asking, "What are you doing these days?" They replied by talking about their current community activities!

Lloyd has been active in scouting for over 60 years. He is a member of the Rotary organization, the Boonton Historical Society, the Rockaway Valley Garden Club (as photographer), was in the Presbyaires singing group for a dozen years as well worked on the Tufts University class reunion committee. Lloyd is an avid photographer, loves to travel and he learned to play trumpet at age 81 so he could appear in Boonton's Santa parade. He went by himself to Gulfport, Mississippi in 2007 to help with cleanup after Hurricane Katrina. Lloyd was awarded the Boonton Citizen of the Year in 2007 and the YMCA Citizen of the Year in 2009. In 2009, he self-published a book, THE ARTISTRY OF BOB BOGUE, about the 20 or so paintings he had commissioned from his lifelong friend Bob.

Don has been the Director of the Presbyaires for the last 15 years. They are a group of about 30 singers who perform bi-weekly at nursing homes. He is a member of Boonton's Historical Society. Also, since his return to Boonton after

145

his retirement, he was the choir director at the Valley Church for many years. Don is a lay speaker and performs Sunday services when called upon to do so. He is currently a member of the choir at the First Presbyterian Church of Boonton, and he is also an elder and lay reader at the church. Since 1991, Don has been playing tennis every day at the Park Lakes Tennis and Paddle Club and for over 10 years he has take part as a member of a local bocci team that plays from June to October each year.

We always count on Don to entertain at Charlton parties, including our wedding day in 2000 when he sang "I Can't Help Falling in Love with You."

In June 2007 we said, "Let's call Don and get him to sing at Lloyd's 80th birthday." Don was happy to do so and even changed the words to the song *"Sunrise, Sunset"* so that it brought tears to our eyes as he sang to his old friend:

Is this the little boy I played with.   When did you grow to be less tall. Wasn't it yesterday - when we were small?"

At Don and Beansie's 60th wedding anniversary this year, Lloyd and I put together a video of these songs and showed the video on a large television screen at the family party at Michelangelo's Restaurant. Don's grandchildren really enjoyed watching the video of their grandfather singing, which they hadn't seen before.

Don participated in the Historical Society program about Bob Bogue in 2007 which ran for 4 months at the museum. In February 2009 he participated in the launching of the book THE ARTISTRY OF BOB BOGUE with Lloyd both at the Senior Center party and also at the Rotary meeting, as well as on Boonton Day.

In the spring of 2010, Boonton High School asked Lloyd if he knew an expert who could give a talk at "Earth Day" at the high school. "Let's call Don," I said to Lloyd. The topic was to discuss what Old Boonton was like before 1903 when the town was flooded to make the New Jersey Reservoir. Since Lloyd was scheduled to talk about rocks and geology, he asked Don to become an expert on "Old Boonton." Don thought Lloyd was crazy but within a few weeks, Don was standing before several high school classes giving his lecture and showing slides of Old Boonton before the Jersey Reservoir.

In June, the third and fourth grade teachers asked for that same talk when the children visited the Historical Society Museum. Then the Rotary Club asked Don to give his lecture for them. Finally, in September 2010, Don was the featured guest speaker at the Historical Society meeting where he shared his expertise on "Old Boonton" once again with a large group of town folk who were knowledgeable about the topic.

Finally, as I review this essay before publication, Lloyd received a telephone call from a local senior residence asking for Don to come and speak to them next month about 'Old Boonton.'

Getting back to the actual interview we had last year, I ran out of time before we discussed their careers. What I do know is that Don had a successful business career as an Assistant Vice President in Continental Insurance Company for whom he worked for 38 years. He is the father of Scott, Kim and Cheryl and he has 3 wonderful grandchildren. Lloyd worked at the Atomic Energy and then as a Test Engineer for Picatinny Army Arsenal. His is the father of Nancy, Bill and Art and has 6 amazing grandchildren.

Asked about old memories, small town kindnesses are expressed in the story Don tells about when his dad, Harold, was a young man skating at the Pond Bridge and Ed Scribner fell through the ice. Harold went into the water and saved this man's life. Years later, when Harold needed work after recovering from encephalitis, Ed gave him a job at Boonton Molding.

In 1936 Don's older brother Whitfield died at the age of 14, after complications from a mastoid infection. "I had a hard time," said Don, "but friends like Lloyd and Bob Bogue (who called me 'little Bro') helped me get through it."

What gave Don some happiness was playing trombone in the high school swing band. He also enjoyed being in the school's marching band and playing in the orchestra. Being the "King" in the Pirates of Penzance was another exciting memory.

Don and Lloyd laughingly recall when Don's grandmother was the President of the local WCTU - Women's Christian Temperance Union. Lloyd would go to Don's house where Don's mother would play the piano while the kids would sing temperance songs. As Don said, "Lloyd came because the refreshments were always good!"

Don loved cowboy serials at Saturday movie matinees. Stories like Buck Jones, Tom Mix or Hopalong Cassidy, were among his favorites. After the movies he and his friends would leave the movie and on the way home they would go through Grace Lord Park. One friend would act the role of Buck Jones, while another boy would act the role of the bad guy, etc. Since hobos sometimes slept at the remains of the iron factory ovens nearby, Don remembers one afternoon in the middle of their fantasy game, a hobo came stumbling out of the ruins and the boys got so scared they didn't stop running until they got home.

Asked about a special toy, both men mentioned getting Lionel trains for Christmas. Lloyd recalled that Santa gave him the exact same set of trains that his older cousin Lee Geier once owned. It was only as an adult that Lloyd realized he must have been given his older cousin's train set.

When I asked if Don had relatives living in Boonton, Lloyd and Don started to laugh because it reminded them of a funny story. It seems Don's grandparents decided to move to Cornelia Street in Boonton and Lloyd said, "My father drove a horse and wagon from Boonton into Brooklyn to move their furniture to Boonton."

Both Don and Lloyd loved radio shows like 'Jack Armstrong,' 'Tom Mix' and 'Bobby Benson.' They remember always carrying a bag of marbles to school but classmate George Zyack would win all their marbles from them.

After his military service, Don went back to visit Boonton High School and asked Mr. Wittman how he could get into college since he had been out of school for awhile. To his amazement, Mr. Wittman tutored Don twice a week for four months so he could pass the college entrance test and he was accepted into Lafayette College that year.

When Lloyd said, "Let me tell one more story" the tape recorder ran out of tape! Anyone coming along in 100 years and watching this 90 minute video will be impressed that the only thing 'senior' about this Dynamic Duo is their 'age.' They are having way too much fun and I bet I'll be interviewing them again in 20 years!

FRANCHI, GLADYS –   Interview 11/30/09 – by Terry Charlton

"Gladys," I ask, "So what's so special about being a senior citizen?" Gladys immediately replies, "Handicapped parking stickers!" This was going to be fun.

Asked about her scariest moment, Gladys said when she was in first grade "I put my tongue on the swing set and it stuck." Gladys could make me laugh every time.

Gladys beams with happiness when she recalls attending school in Boonton. "I was no rocket scientist but I did make the honor roll a few times. I remember if we got passing grades in school we would get a new set of jacks. They cost about 10 cents. That was a big deal." In high school Gladys loved cheerleading for the football team. "You had to get voted on the team (in a school of 900 students) so it was thrilling. And it was nice to go to the games during the day (as opposed to night games that are currently held today). It was so much fun!" she said enthusiastically.

An accomplished cook, a volunteer Catholic Daughter at Mt. Carmel Roman Catholic church, a mother of four, grandmother of 7 and a wife for 44 years to Arnold Franchi, Gladys has a loving connection to Boonton and the many lifelong friends she has made here. Gladys served us tea and homemade angel food cake. Her 22 years working part time at the Reservoir Inn might had added sparkle as a hostess because Gladys makes you feel on first meeting her that you've known her for a long time.

Gladys grew up with siblings Arthur, Svea, Doris and Elsie. They lived on Boyd Street. Gladys also had a sister named Florence who had died before Gladys was born.

In 1934 Gladys' 17 year old brother Arthur was killed in an automobile accident when he was changing a tire on the road. Gladys showed us a treasured end table he made in the Boonton High School woodworking shop. Arthur's wake was held at home and he was buried at Greenwood Cemetery. When her sister Elsie graduated high school shortly after Arthur died, 7 year old Gladys secretly thought Elsie's life would soon be over because Gladys thought that young people died at 18.

Her parents emigrated from Finland but spoke Swedish as well. Her father went to Canada and her mother went through Ellis Island. Her dad placed an ad in the newspaper to find a correspondent from Finland, and after many letters they met in Canada and were married. Her parents moved to New York and during the flu epidemic Gladys remembers her mother telling her, "One day you had a neighbor and the next day you wouldn't have a neighbor." So the Bertells moved to Boonton NJ and Gladys' mother used lots of cleaning products like Lysol to keep her family safe.

"Mama," as Gladys referred to her, was very loving to her children. When the family sat down to dinner if the kids were acting up, she would say, "Papa is looking at you." Gladys recalls, "I don't know why we would think that was a threat because if he ever hit us she would have killed him!" She remembers her mother was a great cook and "Mama could make the most delicious meatloaf gravy ever!"

Growing up in the Depression didn't mean anything to her as a child. Everyone was poor. Everyone helped out at home. You didn't ask for things because you knew better than to do that. To get the 13 cents it cost to go to the State Theater, she returned glass soda bottles to the grocer and she'd get 2 cents per bottle. For a large soda bottle she'd get 5 cents.

Asked what games she liked to play, Gladys remembered that she enjoyed playing Giant Steps, Red Light/Green Light, Hide and Seek, Hopscotch, jump rope, and "I remember going down in front of the Sun Grocery and playing HOME SMASH – hitting a ball – it was like baseball. All the kids would go there until dark." The store was run by Mr. Boyd who was instrumental in getting the first ambulance for Boonton. Gladys said, "After Sunday afternoon dinner my sisters and I would walk up Main Street behind the ambulance and collect money. It is a wonder we didn't get asphyxiated because we were all walking together right behind the truck."

Gladys fondly remembers shopping for penny candy at "Galloways on Grant Street. It was a house. Mr. Galloway was an old man and you walked into his house and I guess it was part of the living room and they put curtains up and he had a candy store and ice cream.

We had a dog that would get loose and in order to get him back we had to give him candy from the candy store. So we would let the dog get loose and then we would say, 'The dog is loose and we can't catch him. We need money to go to Galloways because that is the only way he will come back!' Mr. Galloway was so patient. We would look and look and look at the candy. He would say, "This is good. Everybody seems to like this one. "He was so sweet and patient. He would even break an ice pop in half and sell you half a pop for 3 cents."

Since Gladys didn't remember having a family doctor, I asked her what home remedies her mother used. Gladys told me, "Mama had this cloth and it was from Finland and it was like a magic cloth and she put it on us and she'd say a few words like abracadabra and we'd get well. If we had an earache she would put a drop of warm camphor oil in our ear or she'd put mustard plaster on our chest – and wow that would take the skin off but we all got cured," she said.

She remembers going to Hillary's Pond, Sunset Lake and sometimes they would walk over to Lake Intervale to swim or ice skate. During Prohibition everyone knew about McDonald's 'Still' that was at the lake. "And another thing, they had the Nazi Youth group. They used to go running around the Lake and on Intervale Road way before the war! Nobody thought anything of it. My father used to give them cold water when they passed our house. There were swastikas on the stones after they left."

How did she meet Arnold Franchi? "I flirted with him at a local basketball game." Happily it worked and they were married when she was 21. They raised four children together and she still cries when she recalls how, in their retirement years, they would dance in their kitchen when big band music came on the radio.

"I am thankful to wake up every morning." So what else would you expect someone as jovial as Gladys to say?

A letter to Lloyd from his cousin Lee Geier who lived in Boonton until he was 13 years old.

"Mr. Mann had students recite poems. I remember reciting, "I must go down to the seas again" by John Masefield.

Dr. Wiggins was my favorite doctor. I broke my right arm once and my left arm twice. Guess that's why my penmanship is so lousy.

During the Depression we had a telephone, but we kids were not allowed to use the phone. Too expensive. So I built my own telephone to talk to Doris Crane, next door. Two tin cans and kite string did the job. You had to keep tension on the string or it wouldn't work.

I remember eating tons of green pepper sandwiches. Peanut butter and jelly was too expensive. My mom and some of her lady friends formed a club called "O.H.W.W." which mean "Oh Hell – Why worry!"

Vendors – Mr. Basch delivered "live" fish on William Street every Thursday, and he always bought flounder. Ms. French next door always bought flounder. Mr. Basch would clean the fish before our eyes.

School days – My teacher Ms. Vannetta ripped my threadbare shirt while trying to straighten me up at my desk. I instinctively swung at her and was sent to the principal's office. There was much debate about expelling me. I thought I was a goner. For some reason they decided to put me in an unused classroom by myself. They brought my assignments to me every hour and collected my finished work. This lasted six weeks. Needless to say my grades went up. Looking back on this incident, the only reason I wasn't expelled was my performance in the principal's office. I guess I convinced them my mother worked very hard to feed and clothe me. They never did tell my mother.

Illness? My friend Kenny Osborne stated he was not allergic to poison ivy. To prove it he rubbed poison ivy over his arms, face and ears. I saw him the next day in his bed. I couldn't recognize him. His eyes were swollen shut. His ears and face were swollen and his fingers were six times normal. It took him six weeks to get back to normal. He then came down with scarlet fever. I had mumps and the measles.

Financial help during the Depression

I got a job selling Liberty Magazine. I started out with 10 magazines. A few weeks later I was up to 68 magazines. As an added bonus, for every magazine sold we were given a green coupon – 5 green coupons were exchanged for 1 brown coupon. Accumulating enough brown coupons entitled you to get a free prize gift. I earned my first bicycle. Along with Liberty Magazine, I sold Radio Magazine, Movie Magazine and Physical Culture magazine.

Disaster – the Crash

I was well on my way to making my first million. I had over $200 in the bank when the something hit the fan. The bank closed in 1929. There went my life savings!!

They tell me I haven't been right since the panic.

Guess that's about it. Oh wait!

The first prisoner of war I met was a German captain. He said "The Germans were going to win the War but if they didn't, the Allies would build the place up better than it was before the war." He was right about building the place up.

Love Cousin Lee

GIBIAN, FRAN (SMITH) -   Interview 01/28/10 – by Terry Charlton

Fran is tall at 5' 8", very trim and has a soft voice that is easy to listen to. Fran's strongest asset is her wonderful memory about people in her family. Asked about the Depression, she remembers after the 1929 stock market crash, Uncle Bill lost his house on William Street. A plumber by trade, he had to take a job as a janitor in an apartment building in order to get any work at all.

Her father, Cliff Smith, ran "The Boonton Sports Shop" in the location across the street from the Historical Society (which is now a restaurant). During the early years of the Depression, her mother took in several teachers as boarders at their home on Lathrop Avenue. Then in around 1930, her parents purchased a building at 309 Main Street and her dad opened "Smith's Sporting Shop" where Lloyd (the cameraman for this interview) purchased his first Boy Scout sheath and knife. Fran remembers that her father worked long hours at the store as it was open 7 days a week until 8 p.m.

Fran went to the Legion Building (now the Historical Society) for kindergarten, attended Harrison Street School through 5th grade, and then John Hill School until she went to high school at Boonton High School.

Fran's parents met in an unusual way. They used to skate back and forth on the Canal from Boonton to Dover! And Fran met her husband John at a roller skating rink in Springfield.

Fran remembers that her dad had a bee house with a heater and a stove, and she learned to enjoy 'honey' growing up. Her dad also had a new car that was called a Woody.

Fran loved being a girl scout. She remembers when they hiked through Grace Lord Park together and when they had a Halloween party down by the Falls.

154

Fran must have been very helpful around the house because at the age of 12 she was able to can the pears alone because her mother was sick.

She loved swimming at Clay Hole as a child, and she brought her own three children, Cliff, Gail and Jack to swim at the end of their block where she currently lives on Chestnut Street.

She recalls that where the Town Hall is today there was a firehouse and the firemen used to flood the parking lot so the kids could ice skate. Sleigh riding was also fun on Grant and Harrison Streets and she remembers they used to block off Wootton Street for sledding.

In 1940, after graduating high school, Fran was thrilled to get a job at the telephone company where she earned $13 a week! Her husband John had been in the military in 1937 and had contracted malaria when he was stationed in Panama. After their wedding he worked first as a milkman and then went to Norda (starting pay 75 cents an hour) where he worked for the next 32 years as a truck driver.

Their wedding was at the Reformed Church on Washington Street and their reception was at the Wayside Inn in Denville (the Wayside later burned down). They left for New York City for a honeymoon on Thursday and returned home Saturday. She was thrilled when they went shopping on their honeymoon and purchased a living room set in Macys!

It was with delight that Fran told me that several years ago she was given an award from Boonton and from the State for her 60 years of service in the fire department's women's auxiliary. She is their oldest living member. In my naiveté, I asked her what the auxiliary did, and she replied they have a "calling group" that takes along urns of coffee to the firemen when there is a big fire. They also raise money and collect food to help support needy families in town. And every year at the three-day firemen's carnival held on Labor Day weekend the women's auxiliary volunteer at the concession stands and for many years Fran did that, too.

In 1991, Fran lost her husband to a fast-growing brain cancer. Then in 1999 Fran suffered a heart attack. With bypass surgery and some wonderful medical intervention, she is still doing well 11 years later.

I asked Fran if a sense of humor is important. And she said, "Oh yes! You have to laugh – but you also have to cry." And then she told me about her son Jack and his recent death from a heart attack. She said Jack was born with club feet and required five operations during his early childhood. But Fran didn't dwell on his health challenges, but focused instead on his many successes, including his contributions to the fire department and to his favorite job at Victoria Mews. "He was allowed to do lots of things there and everyone there really missed him terribly. Jack had really found his nitch working there."

An artist with a crochet needle, Fran has made many afghans for everyone in her family, including her 3 grandchildren and 7 great grandchildren.

"I've had a good life and my kids – I wouldn't know what to do without them!" And, with such a loving and outgoing mother, I'm sure her children would say, "I don't know what we'd do without her!"

HALSTEAD, RUTH (DOLAND) - Interview 03/25/10 – by Terry Charlton

Meet Ruth Doland Halstead, a lifelong Boonton resident born on April 1st, 1920. Ruth was quick to assure us, the "April Fool" didn't count because she was born on Easter Sunday. There is a very feminine quality about Ruth, who wore a pink outfit with a dark jacket. She looked fashionable with her nicely styled hair and lipstick that was just the right shade of red. I imagined she would like classical music, but Ruth said she enjoys listening to 'country and western' songs.

Ruth's hobby is painting miniatures and her home was decorated for Easter with lots of hand-painted bunnies. I was captivated by her attention to detail and the intricacy of her work.

Look closely at the boy bunny on the ground level to the left. He is wearing a plum-colored vest, a pink jacket, blue pants, green tie, yellow shirt, with a hat painted in purple with green leaves and a deep pink flower. The bunny is holding an egg in his right hand and it is painted in green, yellow, white and deep pink. In his other hand the bunny holds a bouquet of flowers done with green, blue, dark pink and yellow paint.

157

Ruth remembers as a child she was once given white rabbits for Easter. As I look around her home I wonder if her love for painting figurines was also hatched from that long ago happy memory.

Ruth's daughter Donna Beyer had written a family history and Ruth shared a paragraph of it with me. There is some family lore that a great grandfather received some farm land given by George Washington in payment for veterinarian services during the Revolutionary War. In 1880/81 Michael Doland sold a tract of land to the government, to become a part of where Picatinny Arsenal stands today.

Her father and uncle had a garage on Washington Street (the building is still there) and Ruth remembers the garage had a big fire in 1937. Later her father worked at Wright Aeronautical during the War.

Contrary to many people who were born in her era and only went through eighth grade, Ruth graduated Boonton High School. She recalled fondly participating in the Fashion Club. But when asked if she liked school, she answered succinctly, "Not particularly."

Ruth's mind is sharp as a tack and so it was easy to interview her. She met her future husband at Florham Park roller skating rink when she was a senior in high school. She waited for him for four years when he was in WWII.

When Ruth was 23, her fiancé Perry came home and one week later they went to the parsonage of the Methodist Church on Main Street and were married. The following Saturday her father had a stroke and a week later he was buried. I can't imagine the emotional turmoil this would have created for her, but Ruth is a pragmatist and told that emotional-filled story in a quiet, even-tempered voice.

The newlyweds moved into Madison Street and Ruth's mother always lived with them. There's nothing selfish about Ruth, nor grandiose. She appears to just accept life as it happens.

Through the years Perry and Ruth enjoyed taking many wonderful 'driving' vacations and have traveled to every state in the United States, including Alaska. Sadly, Perry died 25 years ago. On a happy note, Ruth told me that her daughter Donna had three children and now there are three great grandchildren, too.

An only child, Ruth took piano lessons and learned to play well enough to play in the church as background music for the choir. It was delightful to learn that her lifelong friends included Fran Gibian (interviewed 1/28/10) and Marie Werner (we interviewed her son Paul on 2/24/10).

158

Spying a photo of her dad as a member of the South Boonton Fire Department, I asked Ruth if she did any volunteer work, too. She replied without bragging that she was a member of the "Eastern Stars" and rose in the ranks to "Grand Officer for the State." My Internet search indicated that this is a Masonic order that does charitable work and had distinguished members including Eleanor Roosevelt and Clara Barton.

Ruth's memories of childhood in Boonton are happy. There were birthday parties but "Nothing fantastic," Christmas celebrations "We all got together and we still get together," Did she like the Firemen's Parade and Carnival? "It's a tradition."

A vendor she remembers was a 'butcher wagon." I asked that question again because I couldn't imagine such a thing. But Ruth assured me, "I remember him because he always gave me a piece of baloney."

She liked swimming in the Rockaway River down by Monroe Street but did not like ice skating or sleigh riding -- "I didn't like cold air. That's the truth." She recalled that the town closed Boonton Avenue after it snowed so kids could go sleigh riding but again she reminded me, "I did **not** do it!"

Ruth's mother made sure she learned to type and Ruth loved working so much she retired only a few years ago! "I worked at Wright Aeronautical, Western Union for 18 years, Greenson Paper Company for 18 years, and 12 years at the Criminal Management Office at the Morristown Courthouse."

Ruth's philosophy is simple. Enjoy small things like a trip to Walmart with her friend Art, plan a garden umbrella tree featuring her painted bird houses and take life a day at a time.

Ruth's pithy comment sums it all up.

"Age comes along. You learn to deal with it."

HEATON, ALICE (CHARLTON) -Interview 12/31/09 – by Terry Charlton

Alice is the most even-tempered person you'd ever want to meet. Because she had an accident that resulted in a broken hip, Alice is a little slower in step but her mind is sharper than ever. The words, "Dressed for Success" come to mind when you meet her because Alice is always fashionable. Since our interview took place during the Christmas season, she wore a white button down blouse accented with red bias trim on the collar and cuffs. She also wore a long full skirt and matching black knitted vest appropriately adorned with colorful Christmas tree ornament designs.

Alice is the person everyone relies on. Her brother Lloyd (my husband) made sure to mention that Alice graduated high school as a member of the National Honors Society and she was voted in the yearbook as having the "Best Personality."

The Charltons ran a grocery called "The Royal Scarlet" from 1932 to 1946, and she remembers being able to take charge of the store by herself by the age of 13. The cash register they used didn't calculate expenses (or scan and total items as it is done in supermarkets today). Instead, Alice used her mind, a pencil and a list of figures she'd write on a brown paper bag to figure out what the customer owed for his purchases.

Alice was very happily married to Ward Heaton for 38 years. Because of his work, they relocated to Indianapolis and then to Columbus, Ohio where Alice lives today. It goes without saying that Alice and Ward were pillars of their church and community throughout the years and Alice still volunteers with fundraising efforts at her church today. They loved to go camping with their three children, Cindy, Donald and Jeanne.

As far as childhood memories, Alice remembers during the Depression the family grocery story was robbed and the only things missing were staples like sugar and flour. A public telephone was installed in their grocery store and she recalls that a man from New York came into the store and talked on the phone without realizing there would be overtime charges (allotted time for speaking was 3 minutes). When the telephone operator interrupted his phone call and told him he owed a great deal of money, he didn't have the money for the call.

Alice loved Halloween and remembers that when they went 'trick or treating' to the Condit's house they were offered a choice – either a banana or a dime! That was very generous. She said part of Halloween fun was to wear a mask and costume and it was a big secret who you actually were!

Alice recalled that her friend Elaine Padavano got scarlet lever in grammar school and the maintenance man had to wash down her desk and books.

At the current location of Merry Heart, formerly Tallyho senior residence, the Equitable Life Insurance Company owned the building and used it as a Boonton summer vacation location for its employees. This was during the War and travel was restricted. The young girls who came out from New York City loved to swim in the river, rent a canoe at Decker's or walk into town and go to see a movie at the State Theater. Alice said they would often drop by the grocery because it was a neighborhood hangout place.

After high school, Alice went to Bell Labs and, since so many young men were in the military, the Company was willing to train her to become a draftsman and later to run the instruments department.

Alice remembers one thing that I imagine had to be fun for her during the War. Someone put together several trips taking a bus filled with neighborhood teenage girls to the Army base at Fort Dix, NJ to dance with the soldiers!

At the Charlton store her mother formed what they called "The XYZ Club" and put up photos of the neighborhood soldiers in the store window. Many of the soldiers would write to Virginia Charlton, her mother, and her mother would put their letters up on a board so everyone could find out how the soldiers were doing.

161

Asking her to contrast her childhood with that of today's kids, Alice said she believed they were lucky. "We could play – go out in the morning and come back at dinner – and we didn't worry about anything. We could ride our bikes anywhere!" And it seemed there were always lots of kids around to share adventures with Alice.

As we closed the interview, I asked Alice what was best part of being a senior. She smiled, "I'm here! That's enough."

And as for the toughest part? Who else but Alice would say that the hardest part of being a senior citizen?

"Not being able to wear high heels."

HEZLITT, GEORGE AND DOT - Interview 01/08/10 – by Terry Charlton

George is a natural storyteller and Dot has a sense of humor that fits perfectly with his personality. One Christmas he asked her to keep the Christmas tree up because he liked seeing the tree when he came in from work. She not only left the tree set up in the house, he found her hanging fire crackers on the tree on the 4th of July.

"Once when I was young there was a freight train and I was admiring it and the man set me down in the cab and they went 10 feet and it was the darnest feeling. The engineer just touched the throttle and it moved so easily." That event set in motion his love of engines and most especially trains. In fact, George instructed me:

"A **motor** is a device to convert electricity into a mechanical motion."

"An **engine** converts the burning of a fuel into a mechanical motion."

George is loyal. All of his dogs have been given the same name, Nipper. His devotion was an asset during the ordeal he and Dot suffered when their daughter Susan died in a car accident, leaving behind four little girls who ranged in age from 1 to 5 years old. Without hesitation, they adopted the children and brought them up as their own daughters.

Although their home is 30 miles from the coast, Hurricane Charley passed over Arcadia, Florida in 2005. George said their house was demolished. "Then I noticed my travel trailer was not around. Where the heck was it? Well it was out in the back, but it was up in a tree!"

163

George was able to hook up a generator so the pump would work in the bathroom which was, by then, just a toilet with a few walls still standing. Even though it did not have a roof there came a day during cleanup when Dot decided she needed to use the facility. At the most compromising moment, Dot looked up to see a helicopter hovering directly overhead. As she put it, "I was so mad."

George and Dot are so unique and are so remarkably sweet, I had to ask them how they found each other. Dot calmly said, "It was just that there was something completely different about George." George said when he returned from the military, Dot lived next door, and so "Dot was handy. I didn't have to go hunting." That's George – funny!

George remembers he was fed onion sandwiches as a family remedy for intestinal problems, colds and fevers. He now hates raw onions. His first Christmas he and his sister came downstairs to find the tree all set up and decorated with presents surrounding the tree. "We had absolutely no hint it was coming." What a wonderful memory. Each year they looked forward to getting an orange in their stocking. It was an enormous treat!

George and Dot loved to go to Marshalls Barn on Oak Road for square dancing every week. He liked to swim by Ted Witty's property (by the bridge over the Rockaway River upstream from the Powerville Dam).

He believes the insurance man was called Roy Bockman. He would "collect 4 cents for each of us to be insured and he would drive to our house to pick up the 12 cents."

A man came to the neighborhood selling clothing and shoes in the back seat of his car. That's how his family shopped for school clothing. George remembers he would get corduroy knickers and they always made a "squish squish" sound when he walked.

Growing up on Oak Street, George remembers playing baseball and using the mailboxes for the bases. In the wooded area right near his house, "we could run through it and play cowboys and Indians."

George loved radio. One program that impressed him was Dr. Karl Haas, the radio host of the 1950s program called "Adventures in Good Music." Dr Haas said "good music" is in any song – popular or classical – that is still being played 50 years later. George sang to us the song he would like to nominate for 'classic' status:

It was sung by ARCHIE BUNKER …

"Boy the way Glen Miller played, songs that made the hit parade, guys like us we had it made, those were the days.

And you know where you were then, girls were girls and men were men, mister we could use a man like Herbert Hoover again

Didn't need no welfare state everybody pulled his weight, gee our old LaSalle ran great, those were the days!"

Not to be topped by his imaginative memories, Dot said one of her favorite radio programs in the 1940s was called "American Radio Warblers" in which caged canaries were placed near the organ and were heard singing along with the organist.

George said, "If we kids got 25 cents each we would walk down to the town and get a bag of potato chips or a pint of ice cream and eat it on the way home." I wondered if they shared the chips with each other to which George said, "If you didn't have 25 cents, you didn't go with us!"

In grammar school on Powerville Road, he loved a teacher named Bertha Courter, who was also the Principal. Every day she would ask if he did his homework and George would admit honestly, "Didn't do it." When he graduated from grammar school she gave him a $5 prize for making the 'best improvement.' "For years we kids made fun of things she said. Now that I am older, I appreciate all that she taught me."

Giving George a report card on the quality of his recall of old memories and of the entertainment he provided during our interview, like his teacher Bertha Courter, I'd give him a prize for "best loved."

HIGGINS, ELEANOR -   Interview 04/01/10 by Terry Charlton

We met Eleanor Higgins last Sunday at St. John's Episcopal Church where our Presbyterian Church members were sharing a Palm Sunday breakfast get-together with members of her church. Approximately 5 ft tall, Eleanor makes you feel like she is a very old friend. She was born in, and has always lived in, the same house for over 90 years!

Surrounded by some lovely antiques, including a side table that was in Jimmy Holmes' home (before his house became the Holmes Library), Eleanor is a self-proclaimed 'saver' of things. She hates to discard anything because "Maybe I'll need it someday." Eleanor is still holding on to her WWII 'ration books.'

Her dad came to town to work at the Jersey City Reservoir as a derrick engineer. He met her mother at church; they married and settled down to have three children, including her two older brothers, Bud and Harold. When her father took a job with the railroad, if he took a week's vacation he would NOT get any pay so he only took a vacation every five years. Because her dad originally came from Canada, Eleanor remembers they went to the "Thousand Islands" on their vacations because her uncle owned one of the 1000 Islands. "There were four cottages on the Island and we had a wonderful time there!"

Her mother, being of English descent, made plum pudding for the Christmas holidays. Eleanor remembers taking the trolley car (the track was located where the walking path is on Mountain Lakes Boulevard). "You had to take the trolley up to Denville and switch to another trolley to get to Morristown to shop at Epstein's Department Store."

Eleanor said that the Labor Day Parade "Started here on Green Street and would go down and all the way around the Flats (Monroe Street area) and then up Main Street to the West Boonton ball field."

She remembers that "The Richards family had a bobsled and my mother used to say they would go from Gaylord's Gate (way up Boonton Avenue) and they would go down Boonton Avenue on the bobsled down to the Silk Mill building (the building that now has a car on top of the building) and turn around and then they had to walk all the way back. The girls were smart, though. They would talk the fellas into pulling them back up the hill."

The 1933 graduating class at Boonton High School had "Class Night" on the Monday before the graduation ceremony which was held on a Thursday. She was a shy young girl and still marvels that she was able to participate in the show her class performed.

Eleanor remembers friends like Eileen Hopkins, Julia Dunn and Gertrude McCormick. Gertrude had a job with the Fred Weiss Company for 51 years. Lloyd pointed out that Julia Dunn worked at her job for 70 years, and Eleanor chimed in that she worked at Newberry's until she was in her late 70s. The words "loyal" and "hard-working" seem to be synonymous with people from her generation.

I wanted to know what Eleanor 'loved.' She hemmed and hawed – saying she loved movies, enjoyed watching television, attended church weekly … and yet I thought, "Eleanor is so alive and interested in life – there's something else."

Finally, she realized what I was talking about and said "Oh, I know! I am a great Yankees fan! I used to go to the games and I would get in for $.70 cents on lady's day and I went to New York all by myself. And I would get my money's worth by going to double headers. Joe DiMaggio was my favorite. I never saw the Yankees lose. Not once. Double headers and all!"

Suddenly I realized why Eleanor felt like my oldest and dearest friend. She is the kind of person who celebrates other people!

- When I started our interview, Eleanor's first sentence was about how her grandmother was terrific at finding antique treasures at auctions where "Grandmother would sit first row center!"

- And later Eleanor remarked that her mother was an amazing cook.

- Her dad worked hard for his family.

167

- She added, that her friend "Julia Dunn is a wonderful person!"

- And her brother's son "lives in Seattle and they take us to Victoria and Vancouver! I went to the Vancouver World's Fair!"

When Henry B. White said, "He too serves a certain purpose who only stands and cheers," he was probably referring to someone as kind and as loving as Eleanor Higgins!

HORNICK, DORIS -   Interview 11/03/09 by Terry Charlton

Doris was born in her home on 135 Brook Street (now named Boonton Avenue). On her street, there were always lots of friends to play with her.

A typical Sunday would be spent as follows: attending Sunday school, going to church, and then returning home for a pot roast with brown gravy, mashed potatoes and peas. Around the table would be her parents, two brothers and an assortment of cousins and aunts and uncles. Then they'd walk over to Lake Avenue to spend the late afternoon and perhaps have supper with her paternal grandparents. And if it got late, her dad would call Mr. Sims, the taxi man, to take them back to Boonton Avenue. When they walked back from Lake Avenue, the family would often stop at Corvi for an ice cream sundae treat.

Doris admits the boy who worked in Makovsky's Butcher Shop on Boonton Avenue was very handsome. She described him as having "rosy cheeks, black wavy hair and he looked beautiful wearing his white jacket!" They started dating when Marty Hornick and Doris Borgstorm were about 18. A typical date would include seeing a movie together at the State Theater and then having a hamburger at Wormen's ice cream store.

Marty Hornick served in World War II where he was wounded in Germany and received the Purple Heart. Doris said their letters from those war years are safely put away in her attic. Doris remembers their wedding in 1946. It was held in her family's home on Lake Avenue, the house people used to describe as "haunted" because it stood empty for many years before her family moved in. To make the house look more festive for her wedding, she hung new window drapes in the living room – made of 'paper.'

During the Depression, her Dad couldn't find much work as a carpenter so he and her mother opened "Twin Town Bake Shop" in their house on Boonton Avenue. Doris had to help out by learning to cook because as she said, "My mother was working in the bakery." She described herself as a tomboy taking care of her two younger brothers, Einer and Herby. Doris remembers that she would babysit when her parents went barn dancing at Marshalls, or have a night out bowling.

Asked what she remembers about the Depression – she said their family was fortunate. "We were together all the time. We didn't have much meat, but we had food like creamed corn on bread for a treat. We kids didn't know we were poor."

Doris said one of the happiest parts of her life was being a mother to Susan, Christine, Nancy and Marty. She remembers wanting to start a family right away. She loved taking them to the beach on Lake Street and spending many happy hours taking care of them. It was very sad for Doris when Marty died last year. Added to that was the recent tragedy in losing her daughter Christine to cancer.

Always believing in God's protective love, it is with joy that Doris is now sharing her home with her granddaughter Andrea.

Wait – Wait. One of the most important ingredients in this story is missing! Doris Hornick is an amazing musician!!! She has been playing piano since the age of five. I opened Pandora's Box when I asked her where she played music! She played at school assemblies, at school lunchtime dances starting in 8th grade, she played for grammar school performances at the Catholic school, and she played for minstrel shows, the Legion group and worked for 20 years as pianist for the Presbyaires, an ecumenical group that sings old time music in nursing homes in and around Boonton.

During the War, Father Murphy from Our Lady of Mt. Carmel formed an all girls group called MISS AMERICA'S SWING and they played at the Church sponsored "Cross Club," a town youth group. With her mother as saxophonist and her Aunt Emy as conductor, they played for the weekly dances all during the War years. They even performed at the 1939 New York World's Fair!

Asked what a perfect day for her is like, she grins and replies, "Oh, if I accomplish something I set out to do that day – like dust, that makes me very happy."

Asked what she worries about? "Nothing! Not even about me." Asked if she enjoyed her childhood, "It definitely was good. We had a lot of fun!"

A giant sense of humor and an unshakable belief in God's love makes Doris Hornick a charming hostess and a wise, loving and delightful Boonton senior citizen.

Asked what she might change about her life if she could do it all over again, she adamantly replies, "Not a thing! I am perfectly happy." The nicest thing is – that's absolutely true.

LUDWIG, FRED AND HARRIET -

For the Boonton Centennial in 1967 the men in town were encouraged to grow a beard and Fred became one of the "Brothers of the Brush." Since he closely resembles a famous Icon, it's easy to understand why Fred continues to wear his snow white beard. In fact, with Fred's soothing voice quality and natural ability as a storyteller, he resembles Santa more than just by his appearance. He and Harriet have been together for more than 20 years and they complement each other. They love to travel and have been cross-country a half-dozen times. They speak so lovingly to and about each other, they are nice to be around.

Fred grew up on Chestnut Street, with a much older brother Max, and a brother, Paul, who is 15 months younger. From the age of 13, Fred worked in the bakery business. During his career he worked at Paul's Diner for 17 years, and in a part-time business making birthday and wedding cakes for 18 years. Fred also had a bakery store across the street from the original Boonton Diner.

Fred was a real 'find' when it comes to Boonton memories!!!! He talked about building go-carts: starting with a large box, roller skates, a couple of cat food cans for headlights and two pieces of wood for handles.

He remembers that people had 'nicknames.' He was "Fritz" and others were T-Ball, Rudy Toody, Fonzi, Snagger and Old Tipperary. Rudy Toody came to the firemen's parade and would take out a little board and tap dance on it. When someone would give him a shot of whiskey, he would do a handstand to drink the whiskey while on the board.

Fred hated the rubbing sound of his corduroy knickers and would take out his pen knife in school and rub the corduroy until it was flat.

Fred's father belonged to the Odd Fellows Lodge, which was an organization which originated in England and was known for doing charitable work anonymously. The Boonton Lodge met in a hall above the old Post Office at 110 Cornelia Street.

Fred was proud of his father's bicycling hobby. His dad would ride a bike from Boonton to the Bronx, visit with friends, then the next morning ride out to Long Island, ride in a 50-mile bike race, and at the end of the race he would ride home to Boonton.

Halloween? Fred vividly remembers the parade on the playground at School Street School. One year he won a prize for originality. He went as a doctor. He carried a leather bag, wore a derby hat and put together a hose to resemble a stethoscope. For the Parade on Main Street, Fred enjoyed creating his own look! He wore white overalls which he covered with H.O. Oatmeal's box tops and wore a box of oatmeal on his head, while carrying a pot full of oatmeal with a big spoon.

He remembers the family had 65 rabbits during the Depression and every Saturday his father killed a rabbit and Fred's job was to skin it. One Sunday after work he walked in, looked at the rabbit lying on the dinner plate, and swore he would never eat a rabbit again.

With the help of Bobby and Harold McCormick, they would strip the corn silk in their vegetable garden and smoke it.

Fred remembers when Mr. DeCamp owned the Tourne Park and he and the McCormick brothers built a cabin near the top where they would often camp out. In the winter, Fred and his brother Paul would sometimes get up at 5:00 a.m. and go to the top of the Tourne and ski down before school.

At the YMCA in Morristown, Fred remembers the boys were expected to swim nude. Of course it was "boys only" swimming. Harriett remembers in Hackensack the YMCA would issue YMCA bathing suits for swimming.

One game Fred played with his friends was called *Babies in the Hole.* Fred said, "You would get 5 or 6 kids and each one would make a hole and then you'd stand back and roll the ball – if the ball went in the hole – and if you had 5 babies then you would have to stand up against the wall and everybody would throw a ball at you."

Men in town – Bill and Ralph Lucas, Cygon, Christensen - belonged to the Riverside Athletic Club. The would put a plank in the back of a big dump truck and ride up to Franklin Furnace to play baseball. Fred was their mascot. His job was to run after the foul balls and once in a while he would purposely stomp a ball into the ground so he could keep it for himself.

His brother Paul was a good athlete and had a tryout with the St. Louis Cardinals. Paul was invited to come back again when he had reached the age of 18 for a tryout. Instead, since Coach Shriner would not let him pitch on the baseball team, Paul changed to racing. He went with Gerry Hopkins, who was starting a track team, and Paul became the best long distance runner they had! Paul was a "miler." Fred remembers that the team went to the Penn Relays and he remembers that Paul's Boonton team won. Fred made sure to brag that Paul could pole vault almost 12 feet in high school.

Fred's favorite place for sledding was down "Bull Estler's hill." It was named Bull Estler's hill because Don Estler's grandfather owned and lived in the Park House (now a restaurant called Michelangelo's.) My husband Lloyd said he called that hill "Cow Hill."

As for radio, Fred enjoyed:

- The Great Gildersleeve – a pompous bachelor bringing up a niece and nephew.

- Fibber McGee and Mollie where Mollie would implore Fibber not to open the over-stuffed hall closet (a gag they used every week)!

- Edgar Bergen and Charlie McCarthy (a ventriloquist and his dummy). People listening to the radio program *imagined* that Charlie was a real young boy. A typical quip would be W.C. Fields saying:

  "Quiet, wormwood, or I'll whittle you into a venetian blind."
  To which Charlie would reply, "Ooh that makes me shutter!"

On Monday, Wednesday and Friday at 7:30 p.m., the Cullen family would play THE LONE RANGER very loud on their radio. Fred remembers all the kids would stop playing ball outside and would sit on the Cullen porch to listen to the program.

174

Fred signed up for the Navy in 1944 because his older brother Max was in the Navy. Max was transferred from the WASP aircraft carrier to a minesweeper. Just three days later the WASP was sunk.

The War ended when Fred was assigned to a naval ship. He was sent to Japan for two years and he spent that time at Nagasaki where the second atom bomb had been dropped. Fred's assignment? Fred baked.

Once he had grown the beard, Fred would often see small children in the supermarket or restaurant point at him and whisper, "There's Santa." Fred started carrying matchbox cars for little boys and a little bracelet with a bell on it for little girls. When the children approached him, Fred would say, "I know you've been good. Here is a little gift just for you."

Santa, oops, I mean Fred, decided to take his parents on vacation. He remembers how his mother, who had been ill for most of Fred's adolescence, used to squeeze his hand in gratitude while he drove them across the country on a three month motor trip.

Fred told an interesting story. In 1917 Fred's dad worked for a German steamship line that was returning to Germany. Fred's mother was a young German girl visiting her sister in NY. When WWI was declared, his dad's ship was forced to turn around mid-ocean and return to Hoboken NJ because travel between the two countries had been halted! Fred's gift to his parents on their 50th wedding anniversary was a trip back to Germany. The thoughtfulness of this gesture makes me wonder if there really is a little bit of Santa in Fred.

Always in demand to visit nursing homes and assisted living facilities during December, Fred (i.e., Santa) does not charge for his service. "Santa is the person who gives to others," he said.

The aches and pains of being a senior is the only thing he doesn't find "golden" about the golden years. What is the best part? "Why having Harriet with me all the time. I'm the best kept man in Morris County!" To which Harriet quickly responds, "and I am the best fed woman in New Jersey!'

MARSHALL, CHARLIE -   Interview 01/26/10 by Terry Charlton

I can't imagine anyone not liking Charlie Marshall. His name perfectly suits a guy with such an easy temperament, he seems to chuckle as he speaks. Sadly, his only sibling, his sister Alice, died in 1965 after a bout of breast cancer.

Charlie's family is probably best known for MARSHALL'S BARN SQUARE DANCING. The dances were held in the barn near 82 Oak Road, Boonton Township every Saturday night from 1933 to 1958! Women were invited for "free" and men paid "75 cents." His dad Hobart Marshall reasoned, "If we get the women to come, the men will be willing to pay 75 cents to come in, too." Charlie was 6 years old when the square dance business began, and he grew up working at the concession stand. He was able to do square dancing if a group needed another person.

I asked why his family went into the square dance business, Charlie tells this story. It seems Mr. Kanouse built a log cabin down in back of the hotel and he wanted to christen the log cabin and asked Charlie's dad to get a caller and some square dance music to add to the celebration. Half the township turned up and somebody said, "We ought to do this every Saturday night." Within six weeks, Charlie's dad had built the second floor over the barns and was in business.

How did you meet your wife, I ask? "At the dance hall," says Charlie. Mr. Bartholomay used to come up and get Charlie to be a partner with his daughter, Mary "and that's how it began." They were married after he returned from the Korean War and they had three sons. Sadly, their youngest son died a few months ago of cancer.

Charlie worked as far back as he could remember. He cleaned the barn, took care of their seven cows and a team of horses and rode on the ice truck before he was old enough to lift a block of ice. He had jobs on the farm, and worked for his father who had a milk business, an ice business and a wood business. Next door lived Uncle Harvey who was a moving man.

School was not Charlie's strong suit. His mother could be counted on to write a note, "Charles was needed at home." However, he does remember Miss Courter who had three classes in one room – 6th, 7th and 8th. His 8th grade class had 9 girls and 5 boys. It was fun. She encouraged Charlie to write his first book report by encouraging him – then by standing over him to see that he did it. And he found out he liked doing it and finished the requisite 3 book reports required so he could graduate 8th grade.

Another teacher he remembers would write math problems on the board and he would call out the answers at once. His math speed was gleaned from riding on the ice truck every Saturday. I asked Charlie who were their "ice customers?" One customer was Corvi, a shop in town that made home-made ice cream. Another was Drew Chemical where the ice company provided ice for refrigeration of the train cars.

One time a driver for his dad's ice business crashed the truck and ditched it. It was around 1943. Because it was War time and you couldn't get another truck, they had to repair the truck. "It didn't matter how much money you had, you still couldn't get new equipment during the War years."

Charlie came to the rescue even though he was only 15. Because the driver left the company, it was Charlie who had to show his dad where the route and the customers were. "I went 3 days a week with him. And I went to school Tuesday and Thursday."

Charlie served in the Army from 1950 to 1952 and was stationed in Korea as a heavy equipment mechanic. He was also promoted to the rank of Sergeant. They were 100 miles south of the fighting and worked at Kimpo Airport. Because of guerilla fighting, they always had to carry weapons but he did not see combat. The soldiers sometimes at night would shoot their guns in the air and Charlie said it was "a wonder they didn't get hurt."

One childhood memory was very exciting for Charlie. He liked to sleigh ride on his Flexible Flyer and was the best rider in his extended family.

I asked Charlie about playing sports – No. Halloween? "Don't remember dressing up."

177

Movies?

"Never went."

Were you a Boy Scout?

"Never."

Did you go to the carnival?

"We'd follow after the parade to get our truck out of Boonton to go pick up ice in Verona."

"Charlie, I said, "This sounds like a difficult childhood."

Charlie smiled and said,

"I didn't have to go to school.

I got $20 a week and I had no expenses."

Then Charlie added with a chuckle,

"Everything I do – I make it fun or I don't do it."

So what is Charlie doing these days now that he is 82? "I sometimes work at the Valley cemetery." I guess 'Charlie' and 'work' are synonymous. So what else is new?

In 1929 Frank Weiser and his wife, Margaret, parents of newborn Peggy and three year old Gloria, faced the unthinkable. His career as a jeweler in New York City abruptly ended with the Stock Market crash. Compounding that, they were faced with the loss of their home. If that wasn't tough enough, Frank's heartache was magnified when his wife was diagnosed with TB (i.e. tuberculosis). In a time before penicillin, there was no cure for TB and tuberculosis was contagious. Gloria and Peggy had to be sent to live with extended family for several years.

Gloria remembers one vivid memory when she was about 5 years old. Her dad brought her home on a rare visit to see her mother. Gloria's mother stood at the top of the stairs with her arms outstretched waiting to embrace her adored little girl. A year later, Gloria was able to come home permanently after her mother's death.

Gloria Weiser McCormick told me this story when we met on December 21, 2009. Her voice is low and calming. She has a ready smile that lights up her face. Average in height and nicknamed "Weezer" by her friends, Gloria confessed that she referred to someone as an "old lady" and then realized the person she was talking about was her own age.   Gloria also commented laughingly, "I can't remember what I ate for dinner last night, but I remember clearly things that happened when I was five years old." Her lighthearted approach to storytelling made her a wonderful interview subject.

Gloria's father was very strict and he was determined Gloria should become a teacher. She was sent to St. Elizabeth College, but Gloria's vision of happiness was finding a good man, getting married and bringing up a house filled with children. Her prince charming was 20 year old Bob McCormick, her high school sweetheart, who returned after serving three years in World War II. He was a tail gunner and radio operator in the Army Air Corps and his plane was shot down in

Belgium. Bob was able to get back to the front lines two weeks later and was awarded a Purple Heart for being wounded in action.

Bob was also awarded Gloria's lifelong love and devotion. They married in a private ceremony at the Catholic Church. She was 19 and he was 20. "We had enough of the hard times and the sad times. Everybody just wanted to get back to the way life was." Gloria and Bob then went down to her dad's store, the Town Hall Delicatessen, and told him the good news.

The names of her 10 children are a potpourri of popular names of the 1950s and 1960s – Grace, Robert, Kathy, Maureen, Kevin, Michael, Tim, Brian, Eileen and Patty – "And they all turned out to be good people." She adored parenting and has no regrets that she relinquished a business career in favor of motherhood. She did work for 13 years after the kids grew up and left home, but when her husband Bob used to tease her that she "only worked for 13 years," Gloria would pretend to be miffed. After all, raising 10 children and running a household for 12 people felt like real work to her!

Her father Frank remarried about a year after his wife's death. His jewelry skills were a perfect match for a job at Aircraft Radio Corporation and they moved to Boonton in 1938, when Gloria was 12. Ultimately, they bought a 15 room house on Rockaway Street in the Park Section of Boonton. "We kids hated that house. It was pretty rundown. There was even black wallpaper in one of the rooms." Ultimately, her father opened a store called the Town Hall Deli which was located across the street from the Historical Society building.

Asked about her memories of adolescence in Boonton, Gloria remembers her family shopped at the A&P on Washington Street. She liked the 'XYZ Club' formed by her best friend Alice Charlton when they hung out at the "Royal Scarlet," a grocery store owned by Lloyd and Alice's parents, Virginia and Frank Charlton.

Gloria remembers going to Division Street once a week and folding bandages for the Red Cross as part of the War effort. She loved listening to the *Inner Sanctum* on radio and watching classmates get tested yearly for TB in school. (She received a chest x-ray because of her family history.) She remembers that the English teacher, Ms. Edwards, didn't like boys wearing suspenders. She was a stickler for respectful behavior in her class, too.

Gloria went to the State Theater on Saturday afternoons and recalls the ticket seller's name was Gilda Miccioni. She remembers Halloween costumes were not purchased at a store! She wore long skirts, baggy sweaters (the bigger the better) and saddle shoes when she went every Friday night to dance at the Cross Club (run by Mt. Carmel church).

She tells the story that during World War II they sold margarine with a yellow bead that had to be broken open inside the plastic white margarine bag. This was done to change the margarine to look yellow like butter. To this day, Gloria hates margarine.

Bob McCormick was a volunteer fireman. Gloria went to the Catholic Church "Rosarian" meetings. "Oh, you volunteered?" I asked to which she admitted, "It was also a night out" and they both looked forward to that!

Predictably, when asked what marvels of the 20th century she most enjoyed – Gloria replied "it was the automatic washer and dryer!" Of course, having a second bathroom in a family of 12 was lovely, too. But there was a time when the kids were little when Monday meant wash day - all day - in a time of cloth diapers and big families, Gloria remembers wash day meant:

A   putting laundry in a tub with an agitator that swished the clothing around in soapy water

B   wringing the clothes manually through the spinning wringers into cold rinse water

C   then again agitating the clothing in clear water to remove the soap

       (diapers with soap residue meant babies with severe rashes)

D   then wringing the clothing again – sometimes twice to remove the water

E   hanging the clothing outside on a clothes line summer and winter

F   bringing the clothing inside at the end of the day – and in winter that meant bringing in frozen clothing that would need to be thawed at the radiator

I was most struck during the interview by Gloria's unwavering belief in a loving God.

Religious-oriented "terrorists" in today's world believe a loving God expects them to combat the evil in this world by blowing themselves up along with hundreds of innocent bystanders.

I prefer Gloria's God.

MC GLONE, JIM -

It is rare to meet a person who can boast that he has spent the last 52 years doing work that he performs exceedingly well and that he loves! Added to that, he actually gets paid to do it, too! Meet Jim McGlone, a lifelong Boontonite. He is a Professor of Speech and Theater at Seton Hall, a Catholic university located in East Orange, New Jersey. He has another distinction! Besides having written a book about Ria Mooney, a Director of the Abbey Theater in Ireland, Jim brags that his four children, their spouses and his 16 grandchildren all live nearby! That isn't just luck or rare good luck – it's an absolute miracle in today's modern age.

Jim has a very easygoing style of conversation. Of average height, Jim is intelligent, quick-witted and charming, too, with humility not usual in a person who has a doctorate from NYU. In describing himself, Jim said he got one of his mother's best traits -- her "tenacity." The Thesaurus describes that as: determined, stubborn, undaunted, industrious, insistent and resolved. Since part of Jim's career is to research and direct plays written by Irish playwrights, he was especially lucky to have the "tenacity" to pursue his very unique dream.

Born at home in the early 1930s, Jim and his brother Joe had a happy childhood. Jim's mother, while born in Boonton, spoke only Slovak until she was six years old and so she was a very intelligent but shy and private person. She was also a gifted seamstress.

Jim's dad worked at Van Raalte and was a kind, good-natured man who taught his sons to respect their elders. His father had one rule, "You either go to church or you are dead." Since Jim loved the pageantry of Catholicism and was an altar boy for many years, this was an easy rule to follow. Jim's dad came from an era where a man never stepped into the kitchen, never went shopping and wasn't very handy around the house either. (I suspect the apple hasn't fallen far from the tree regarding those traits in Jim.)

Jim began performing at the age of 6. He recalls that he had lots of opportunity in Boonton to perform. He was in productions staged by Father Murphy at Mt. Carmel, he appeared in the American Legion Minstrel shows and he was part of the Mountain Lakes Dramatic Guild, which is now the Barn Theater Group. Ann Apgar Reeves, a school friend, told me that she remembers how Jim loved performing in high school plays and what fun they had as young teenagers going into New York City to shop for the fabric needed for everyone's costumes. Perhaps his love of directing started in those high school productions.

In the late 1930s, when the Depression was deepening, Jim said his parents were considering moving from the house that they rented. Instead, the landlord lowered their rent. I remarked at how surprising that was but Jim assured me, "People in Boonton are like that. They are kind."

Growing up 'Boonton' – there were always lots of kids in the neighborhood ready for a pickup game of baseball or football. As they grew into adolescence, Joe and Jim were allowed to go anywhere in town because Boonton was safe. They'd swim at Hillary's Pond or Clay Hole even though there were never any lifeguards because they were always surrounded by lots of friends. Not many automobiles were in use in the 1930s, so sleigh riding down Hill Street was great fun, too. Kids always knew that if a neighbor saw you step out of line, there would be a telephone call to your mother -- and no one wanted that to happen! !

Jim is a 'people' person and takes pride in the fact that he knew everyone in town. If he had to choose another career, Jim said he would run a restaurant or ice cream shop so he could hang out with the town folk. He remembers fondly when he would go to Alfie's store he would answer the phone (using a parody of the "Duffy's Tavern" opening lines in its radio show):

"Hi. Alfie's place where the elite meet to eat. I am the manager. Alfie ain't here!"

The town was divided into the Flats, Park section, Cabbage Hill and West End, and his friends included kids whose parents immigrated from places like Germany, Italy, Czechoslovakia, Ireland and Austria. With such a rich diversity of cultural backgrounds, Jim mused, "We never talked about it." Jim developed this unspoken philosophy as a child -- just because a person has a different upbringing, it doesn't mean that they can't be your friend.

Asked how he came to love acting, Jim said that "A lot of my love for space, color and form come from my religious experiences." As an altar boy, Jim loved the

Christmas pageantry with Midnight Mass, beautiful organ music, glowing candles, incense burning and the large red bows worn by the altar boys.

Jim's enthusiasm for all things 'tradition' even colors his yearly birthday celebration. Jim's daughter uses her grandmother's recipe and every year he gets to have the exact same thing - chocolate cake with butter icing.

Around 1985 Jim had 3-way bypass and so when I asked him what he especially liked in our modern world – television? -- computers? -- cell phones? – Jim was quick to remark the miracle of 'modern medicine' is what he likes best! Asked what he loved best about this time of his life? His answer was immediate --- his 16 grandchildren! "I am a very lucky man!"Frankly – I have to agree with him!

Bill Nikel graduated Boonton High School in 1944 at the age of 16. "If I had my life to live over again it wouldn't happen that way. I skipped two grades in grammar school which put me out of sync socially." But it couldn't be helped. Billy was a precocious child surrounded by achieving adults. Anyone who earns an advanced degree in marketing from the Wharton School of Business is definitely gifted.

Frank Banta, his grandfather, loomed large in his young life. "He was great. He knew everybody in town and probably lent money to half of them. He was so good-hearted." Billy's mother was equally as good hearted and he loved to play 500 Rummy with her. She encouraged him to go to college. But it was his granddad who was his real hero. "He would sneak down in the middle of the night and get a peach out of the serving bowl." That was absolutely verboten to Bill's mother. She was a strict adherent to Emily Post's rules on proper table etiquette.

I liked Bill Nikel when I met him because he was excited about the project Lloyd and I have initiated in capturing the oral histories of Boonton seniors. Bill is trim and athletic. He likes to hike, he still loves to ride a bike and he is actively involved in activities at his retirement community in West Caldwell. Bill brought along to our meeting a photo and momento album about his mother's life done by a caregiver years ago (before scrapbooking became an art form). What caught my eye was a 1967 receipt for a brand new 1968 Chevell automobile that cost $3,632.

Growing up in Boonton, "I was crazy about bikes. I had a Rollfast and a Schwinn." He also loved his dog Oscar who used to guard Bill's bike when he was in high school. He loved the 7th grade math teacher, Mr. Champion, who had two boys in his class named Bill. The teacher solved the problem by calling one of them

"Billy, the Kid" and the other, "Sheriff." He has fond memories of being in the chorus in the school performance of "The Pirates of Penzance."

Bill enjoyed "The Lone Ranger" on radio. At the movies, he enjoyed "The March of Time" and the serial called "Buck Rogers." In 1938 he saw the "Son of Frankenstein" at the State Theater and remembers being scared as he walked all the way to his house in the Flats. The story went like this: The blacksmith Ygor (Bela Lugosi) finds the monster's ailing body and heals the monster (Boris Karloff) only to discover the legends about the monster are a reality!

Bill's story about his summer in Maine made me wish I could have gone on that vacation, too. He recalled, "The best vacation I ever had was with my mom. We went up to Maine to a town called Naples on Long Lake and we stayed at the Chute Homestead. We slept in a tent on a platform. We had meals at the lodge. They had a recreation hall. The place was fantastic. There were tennis courts and swimming. On Saturday you'd go out in a fancy boat and you'd go to an island and have cookouts."

Asked about his memories of Boonton, Bill tends to talk more about work than about adventures. With his friend Butch Lewis, they put an ad in the local paper that they would do odd jobs. The first job they got "was pulling weeds for what seemed like months but was probably only a couple of days. That cooled our ardor for odd jobs." (Dear Reader, I am using Bill's language as he is an excellent public speaker and storyteller.)

Bill had a paper route for "The Star Ledger." He sold magazines for "The Saturday Evening Post." He also worked at "The Sweet Shoppe" with his friend Ed Force.

The job that most intrigued me, though, was when Bill sold Fuller Brushes. Being intelligent, hard working and comfortable talking to adults, Bill was a natural for this job. He remarked enthusiastically, "I loved it!!! I had a big basket on my bicycle and I would put the sample case in it and knock on a door and I would say, *'Well, Madam, I have this gift for you. Here's a lapel brush.'* And another gift was a little red plastic comb. This is what you call 'door-openers.' A fiber broom was $1.19 and the big ones were $1.69. Trying to deliver the large brooms and mops, I had to ride one-handed on my bike and hold the broom out in my other hand."

In the 1940s, considering that all young men were being drafted for World War II, Bill probably has the distinction of being Boonton's youngest Fuller Brush "boy!"

Meeting Nola on a blind date, he said he felt love at first sight. He thought she was so "loving and kind" and he still admires how she always reaches out to others. They have four children Andrew, David, Nell and Julie and a handful of grandchildren whom they love very much.

Bill's career in marketing and market research was varied and fascinating, but he also enjoyed being in the Naval Intelligence during the Korean War where he was "trained in doing security investigations, which was really plain clothes work. I loved doing that!"

As we ended the interview I asked Bill what was the best part of being a senior citizen. Bill replied immediately and emphatically, "The grandchildren!"

Bill Nikel has the distinction of being born in 1928, the same year as "Mickey Mouse." Mickey can boast that he is an adorable comic cartoon but Bill's claim to fame is that he is a family man who has brought his ethics and character to the work place and who still contributes to others through a group he co-founded over 20 years ago called "Job Seekers of Montclair." Hey Bill, I want to give you a "shout out" for your volunteer activities that have helped others help themselves.

OSTERHOUDT, ANN (BARNISH)   Interview 03/01/10 by Terry Charlton
With daughter and son-in-law, Onnolee and Carl Allieri

"I always liked Boonton. I thought Boonton was a nice, clean place to live." With such a ringing endorsement from a resident who has lived here for 106 years, that's saying something.

Accompanied by her daughter and son-in-law, Onnolee and Carl Allieri, Ann seemed delighted to let us spend the afternoon talking to her at Merry Heart senior residence. As we sat facing each other, I kept thinking, "How many people ever get to meet a person who is over 100 years old, let alone to 'interview' a woman who is currently 106 years old?" I felt it was such a privilege to meet Ann Barnish Osterhoudt who was born September 28, 1904. Ann told us her parents came from Poland and Czechoslovakia.

Ann told her son-in-law Carl, when she worked packing margarine at The Wacoline (later E.F. Drew) she would go outside the building and rub her face with the 'stuff' that came out of the chimney stack. Perhaps that is why her skin is so beautiful it actually glows. Aside from having trouble with her hearing, Ann appears to be the picture of health. She's trim, pretty and she has perfect posture. Her mind is wonderfully sharp for a person who has lived currently 106 years, and Ann is very friendly, open-hearted and gracious.

As a young girl, Ann worked at Van Raalte "making stockings."

Meeting Ann, I was reminded of a ceremony we attended last week when the Boy Scouts celebrated their 100th anniversary. Incorporated in 1910, the scout laws reflect the integrity expected from people of Ann's generation.

BOY SCOUT LAWS:

TRUSTWORTHY	**COURTEOUS**	**THRIFTY**
LOYAL	**KIND**	**BRAVE**
HELPFUL	**OBEDIENT**	**CLEAN**
FRIENDLY	**CHEERFUL**	**REVERENT**

Religion has always been a very important part of her life – "Before we went to bed – all us kids – stood at the table together and prayed." There were 13 kids altogether and Ann proudly announces, "And all of us were born in the house." Onnolee said that Ann remembers a midwife with a surname of Scozzafava who helped with the births.

Ann remembers "Dr. Hornick. He delivered a lot of babies and he was one nice fella and everybody loved him."

Ann didn't like school very much because she knew she was needed at home. She left St. Mary's (now Mt. Carmel) after 8th grade. Her mother took in the laundry for Mr. Dawson's family and Ann did all the ironing. Mr. Dawson had a lumberyard on Division Street.

Ann doesn't recall her childhood as a time of deprivation. While she didn't have many toys, she did not once mention that. Instead, she recalls vividly, "***There were a lot of neighbors and some of them were so poor I felt sorry for them. It's a shame how they had to suffer.***" So Ann and her mother prayed for others and helped those who were less fortunate.

What gave her pleasure were the roses her mother grew "from a cutting!" "They were "**so beautiful**" Her mother would say, "Now we can pray together and ask God to help us to make other people who are sick – to make them well."

Brought up on Union Street, she tells the story that, "We had a coal stove in the cellar so I went down to the train station and picked up coal and put it in pails to bring home for our fire in the stove." Her father worked at the nail factory. Ann remembers the Company "gave my father and mother a garden so they could plant vegetables so they could have it for the kids." The company (Fusee) was located on the corner of Morris Avenue and Fanny Road.

Ann remembers when her brother caught a bunch of fish; the two of them went around town selling the fish for 25 cents apiece. When her brother swam out and got lily pads in the water, "we sold them, too." In fact, "I used to sell bananas because the banana man's wagon didn't stop at everybody's house."

Her favorite stop was at Gillacki (phonetic), an ice cream store by the railroad station "That was the only place in town where you could buy an ice cream cone. It cost 7 cents and a lot of kids went down there."

Ann also recalls that she went to the Giant Supermarket. "I had to go down there and get a few things, too, because it was cheaper."

One of the games Ann remembered playing as a child she called 'Peggy' – and it had to do with taking two flat sticks, making pencil points on each side of the stick, and then getting another stick and hitting them.

"My mother let me go to the Lyceum once in a while to see the movies." When I asked how much it cost, she laughed, "We didn't pay anything. They let us go in for free because my mother had a lot of kids."

Marrying later in life, Ann eloped as she "didn't want a big wedding." They honeymooned at Niagara Falls and, typically, Ann recalled, "It was very nice but I just couldn't wait until I got home!" Ann now has two daughters, two sons-in-law, 9 grandchildren and 15 great grandchildren. Everyone still relies on Grandma to pray for them, especially at test time in school or when taking a trip.

Amazingly, Ann has never taken prescription medicine in 106 years! She was never sick as a child. For home remedies, she does remember her mother wrapped Vicks in a stocking and hung it around Ann's neck. And she told us she ingested Vicks. She even told us she was fed a teaspoon of kerosene! "It doesn't taste bad."

Carl and daughter Onnolee came home one night after Ann had been babysitting and their house 'stunk'. It seems their son David had been running a high fever and Ann used a traditional home remedy of applying onions to help break his fever.

Ann starts to laugh and says, "I remember a policeman – Gilmartin. **He's old!!!!** He was Chief of Police." She smiles and says, "Well at least you had a little laugh." Then she licks her thumb and rubs it against her shoulder, "When you are doing something good – put a medal on your shoulder."

At the close of the interview I went up to Ann and took her hand while I thanked her. Ann smiled and said, "Let the Lord help you and your family."

I felt her blessing for my family and it was a lovely gift from an amazing woman.

PERRY, DIXIE (ASPERINA CROCE) - Interview 03/14/10 by Terry Charlton

Asperina "Dixie" Perry is diminutive, standing no taller than 4' 10" and probably weighing no more than an average 10 year old today. She lives on her own and did all her own yard work until she broke her hip two years ago. Boasting is not something Dixie would do. However, she is a fine seamstress, proud of her family, a hard worker and a devoted Catholic.

Asperina (called DIXIE by her friends) was born at home. Dixie recalls that her house was once converted to a hotel.

Like many young people of her era, Dixie only went through the 9th grade in school because she had to "help the family." She helped the family by cleaning houses, working at the 5 & 10, working at an umbrella factory and making $8 a week at Van Raalte.

Her parents came from Italy as young adults. "There was this candy store – the Londons – they were Jewish people – near Johnny's Tavern and my mother learned a lot from these people. They were very nice. We might have lived upstairs."

Dixie's father worked at whatever jobs he could get. She remembers "Wherever there was dirt, pipes, cement or bricks to handle, he would be working. He worked for E.F. Drew and he would be up in a chopper, or down in a ditch."

Dixie's mother was very good at sewing and she made the children's clothing. She also tried making a mattress and she used chicken feathers to make pillows. She even made the family's soap. Dixie remembers, "My mother made her own sausage. She was an excellent cook." She recalls a delicacy called "Squab" which I believe she said was made with pigeon meat.

The only time Dixie had her picture taken was for the class photo from her 8th grade graduation. Other childhood memories include watching her brother build a wooden wagon and Dixie and her sister riding on a scooter.

She recalls a vendor who came around with his pet bird – maybe it was a parrot. After giving him a penny or so, the parrot would go over to a box and pick out a card that had your fortune on it.

It must have been a very early memory, because Dixie vague recalls that after the Iron Works ended there was something called "The Bronze Works" in the Hollow. Lloyd said that the Bronze Works was close to the town garage and recycling center. What stands out in her mind was how the men carried lunch pails and "all had dust on their shoes."

Her younger brother Willie accidentally drowned at age 21 at Deep Hole. "In those days you were 'waked' at home" and her mother insisted Willie be laid out in a tuxedo. Dixie remembers it like it was yesterday. It was so incredibly sad. Her knees were shaking when she came into the room. Her mother took it very hard and Dixie herself still fills with tears when Willie's name is mentioned.

Her brother "Corky" had something wrong with his foot when he was born and Dixie believes it was caused by polio. He worked as a barber in town. When everyone raised their haircut prices, Corky didn't and everyone came to his shop. Lloyd remembers as a small child that if he sat still and didn't wiggle, Corky would give him back a nickel after the haircut.

Dixie remembered she came home with lice in her hair and "Oh, how my head itched!" Her mother used a fine tooth comb to get rid of the lice and the girls had the shiniest hair in school. For her First Communion, Dixie's mother took her to a beauty parlor to get a special type of wave in her hair called a Marsella (phonetic). When Dixie got in the tub that night she stuck her head under water and ruined all the newly created waves in her hair.

Instead of Halloween memories, Dixie talked about how Italian people in Boonton celebrated Mardi Gras (the day before Ash Wednesday). Her parents would dress up and go from house to house and there was music and everybody cooked something. "Oh, the goodies!"

Speaking of music, Dixie loved to dance and remembers fondly that she and her friends would go into New York City and dance at Roseland. She said "We even wore gowns at the Elks when they held dances. It was wonderful."

A childhood game described by Bill Bednar in his interview had to do with a person standing against a building wall (according to Dixie, this person was called the "pillow"). Then three or four people on the team would bend over and lean up against each other and against the 'pillow' in a chain.

The opposing team of 3 or 4 people would then jump on the chain and try to get the chain of kids to collapse. Instead of being chosen to be the "pillow" person who got to stand against the wall, tiny Dixie was put into the chain of kids being jumped on. She says, "No wonder I have a bad back today!"

Dixie always sat up right next to the man who played the piano as she watched silent movies. She remembers collecting an entire set of pink dishes at the State Theater on dish night. She told me she still has those dishes packed away and still not used. She was married in1943 and her husband has since died.

There is a saying: "These are the golden days!" According to Dixie, "Well – they aren't!" There are aches and pains associated with being a senior citizen!

Lloyd commented, "What's golden is that it takes so much gold to get through these years!"

Thus ended a wonderful interview, full of laughter and great stories thanks to our charming interviewee, Dixie Perry!

REEVES, ANN (APGAR) -   Interview 04/09/10 by Terry Charlton

    Don't expect "somber reflections" when interviewing Harry's wife Ann Apgar Reeves. Ann is forever young and very petite. Ann and Harry are devoted to each other and Ann talks with a mother's pride about her four beautiful daughters. Her family is her first canvas.

    Ann's innate artistic talent has been honed by years of painting and her artwork is well known in New Jersey. The range of her interests include painting "The Berlin Wall," which is hanging in the Berlin Museum, to commissions she receives from different Towns in New Jersey to create historical town paintings. Ann's paintings are visual stories – delightfully and descriptively narrative in content. Comparing her work to my favorite painters, I see touches of Renoir's joy in her choice of subjects and Rafael's assurance of color in her vivid paintings.

"September 11" painting

"Palisades Park" painting

194

Below is a work we commissioned in 2010 entitled "Our Back Yard" and it depicts the fun and happiness we share as the Charlton clan when we get together. From bocci, to a swimming pool, to archery, badminton, playing music, to celebrating an engagement announcement in front of the gazebo – and with the grandchildren playing in the driveway - this painting is full of sunshine and happiness.

Ann's dad was a carpenter with a passion for sailboats and gliders. His boundless creativity rubbed off on Ann. He even built the family home. Ann's mother was only 16 when she married. Ann and a brother born 11 months later soon occupied her mother full time.

Ann tells the story of how her parents encouraged her creative talents. There are photos dating back to her fifth birthday showing Ann drawing and painting pictures. Because of her interest in fashion, she was given a sewing machine as a teenager. When her dad's boat needed a new canvas sail, Ann said, "It never dawned on me that maybe I couldn't make a sail. I just did it because he thought I could do it! And my mother was the same way. She thought I was great at everything I tried."

Ann Reeves grew up in Parsippany and attended Boonton High School. Asked if Ann played sports, she recalls that soccer was just being introduced in gym classes and she loved soccer but she wasn't very athletic. Then she went on to describe the "balloon" shorts they had to wear in gym and how they were not flattering to full-figured girls.

Friday in school was called "Dress-Up Day" and Ann thought that was wonderful because she could wear her "silver long dress with silver ballerina shoes or her lavender lace dress with platform shoes!"

Ann dreamed of someday becoming a fashion designer and after winning a scholarship to fashion school in New York City, she was one of two finalists for a job at Vanity Fair, "But they took the other girl because I was engaged and they figured I'd go and get married."

"Question?   And were they right?

ANN: Yes.   If you wanted to be a 'career girl' you didn't get married.'"

In a time before college degrees and birth control methods, women were expected to be nurses, mothers or teachers – and those who aspired to having more challenging careers were very often childless.

Ann was soon parenting four little girls, the oldest being 5 years old. She admits those were rough years because Harry was developing his career and often worked at two jobs. "Thank God for my mother and mother-in-law. They helped me out. Otherwise I could have gone bonkers."

Asked about her fondest memories of Boonton, Ann waxed poetic:

"I took a school bus to Boonton High School. I loved it! It was like being in heaven with all the social things. I loved the school bus! I loved all the kids!!!   And I loved, loved, loved walking uptown and going to Newberry's or Woolworth's 5 & 10. There was Shirley's Dress Shop and some shoe stores! I was in heaven. I envied kids who lived in Boonton because they could walk into town every day and they could see each other every day."

Then Ann went on, "Oh!!! The houses! To me they looked like mansions! They had these porches with lights on them and I think that's where I got my love of painting houses. I fell in love with the Town!"

Admittedly, not much of a student, Ann said, "I dreamed away during high school. I wasn't good at math so that showed, but in history and English literature I used to draw fancy brochures and pictures and I fooled the teachers into thinking I was learning something."

After school she looked forward to going to the Sweet Shoppe and having a hamburger and a chocolate soda with friends! It is easy to imagine Ann must have been very popular. She wasn't the self-conscious type. She probably didn't worry about whether she would 'fit in.' In fact, I cannot imagine Ann worrying about things like that at all. What I can imagine is feeling her warmth and obvious pleasure in meeting a new person.   I can almost hear her saying something like, "I'm so happy to meet you!!! I really want to get to know you!!! I just love what you are wearing!!!"

Ann recalls fondly, "I took part in all the plays in Boonton High School. There was a guy named Jimmy McGlone [now a director of theater at Seton Hall] and we used to go into New York City's garment district and buy fabric and I designed the costumes for the plays!"

"Were you good enough to make the costumes?" I gasped? To which she replied, "Probably not – but I did it because I thought I could."

Winding up our interview, I asked Ann what was the hardest part of being a senior citizen. "Not being able to wear high heels!" Now who would have guessed that.

And the "best part of being a senior citizen?"

"I feel a peacefulness. You've done what you wanted to do and you don't have to try anymore. You can just enjoy life."

I asked Ann what gives her 'joy' -- not including her family or painting.

Ann was quick to reply, "Just looking out the window every day – the birds, a tree - it doesn't take much."

And so the meeting ended and Ann was free to go back to her easel!

We lost count of how many times we laughed during the 45-minute interview with Ann. What we did agree on was that she was not only loving and talented but she is also a thoroughly delightful person.

REEVES, HARRY -   Interview 02/20/10 by Terry Charlton

Married in 1954 to Ann Apgar Reeves, they share an interest in cooking is shown in their kitchen by the decorative touch of hanging 28 cast iron frying pans. Also, their home reflects their love of antiques. Their extensive collection of Tiffany lamps add beautiful moments of color throughout the house.

In 1998, when they decided to move to a smaller home in Belvidere, NJ, Harry immediately added a sun-filled, enclosed and heated back porch so Ann would have the perfect setting in which to paint.

This interview is about Harry Reeves, the person who makes it all happen for Ann. Harry was born in a house on West Main Street (currently occupied by the Jim Carroll Insurance Agency). An only child of Olive Charlton and Harold Reeves, With a dad named 'Harold' and his grandfather named 'Harry', it was easy to guess his nickname would be 'Junior." Harry appears to be a very easygoing man, reliable and quick to see the humor in everything. Harry exhibits the steady confidence of a person who enjoys life and who achieves whatever he sets out to do. Despite the seriousness of undergoing two open heart surgeries a few months ago, Harry characteristically shrugs off any health concerns. "I wasn't worried."

Harry's dad worked at the silk stocking factory, Van Raalte, for 20 years. Harry remembers there were three stages to making a silk stocking – the topper, the footer and the legger. As a four year old being taken into the factory, Harry was amazed at "How big the machines were." During WWII, silk was needed for parachutes and so the factory closed its doors permanently.

My husband Lloyd remembers Harry's mother Olive (his first cousin). Harry described his mother as both intelligent and creative. She even worked for a newspaper at one time. Grandpa Harry, who lived next door, was "kind of gruff." He was prominent in town as Director of one of the banks, and for a time he was

President of the School Board. He owned his own oil company called Charlton Oil (later sold to Dixon Brothers).

Asked about childhood illnesses, Harry remembers he might have had rheumatic fever – at least he distinctly remembers being in bed for six weeks. Harry said even though penicillin was discovered in 1936, during the early War years it was not available because it was needed for the troops. He remembers a young boy who lived across the street died of leukemia which was a fatal disease at that time.

Harry said his parents were not strict. They had certain unspoken family rules. "Once the sun came up I could go anywhere. I just had to be home before the sun went down." And what he wanted was to play saxophone in high school for 4 years, climb up on Indian Rock, work at Guiton's Gas Station (opposite Del's Village) and attend the Saturday matinee at the State Theater where he enjoyed Gene Autry movies. He loved swimming down by River Road and Chestnut Street because there was a big tree "with a 100 ft rope" hanging over the water and the water wasn't muddy.

Harry remembers Halloween with delight when he would get dressed in costume to ring doorbells and get candy. "For the last 2 years I went to every single house in town!" It got so that people would say when he arrived to collect candy, "We wondered when you were coming."

His choice in radio programs included Gangbusters, Ellery Queen, The Phantom and FBI in Peace and War.

He was only about 7 years old and visiting relatives in Middletown, NJ when suddenly the whole neighborhood came alive with people shouting out their windows, "Pearl Harbor got bombed." He knew what a bomb was! As for Pearl Harbor, he reasoned it must have been "a big basin lined with pearls."

With his sharp memory, Harry rattled off the names of his teachers – Mrs. Spender, Jennie and Carrie Davidson ("they lived on Liberty Street" and walked to school), Ms. Morrissey, Ms. Wicks, Emily Davis, Ms. Sutton, Ms. Kelsey, and the lady who pulled on her strap, Ms. Leonard. He recalled Ms. Vreeland pulled wax out of her ear and Ms. Teague, who taught English, was picked up by a 6'8" student (who played on the basketball team) and put in a garbage can because she was acting prissy. The boy got suspended.

Harry was proud to be a crossing guard wearing a badge that he thinks might have said "Police Patrol."

During his business career Harry worked as a district manager in QuikChek and in other retail stores. The work required travel, long hours and lots of pressure. So what did Harry do for entertainment? Why he went into local politics in Hackettstown and was on the Town Council for 9 years.

Harry was going down the "up" staircase in high school when he literally bumped into the girl he would someday marry. When he saw her again at the Steve's Sweet Shoppe, he asked her to go to the prom. Ann said 'yes' as she needed a date for the prom and "He looked like a nice guy." He was obviously nice because they got married and went to live in California where he was stationed in the Navy. So began a marriage in 1954 between two people who are still very much in love with each other.

As we closed the interview, I asked Harry, "What is best about being a senior citizen?"

Humorously, Harry replied, "I don't get up for work at 4 a.m. anymore."

SCOZZAFAVA, TONY -   Interview 07/29/10 by Terry Charlton

    While serving in the Navy in the early 1960s, Tony Scozzafava was assigned
to the aircraft carrier USS Hancock CVA19. He said:

    "We were going into dock in Hawaii and we were all lined up on deck in full
dress uniform. … It was so quiet as we slowly passed the ARIZONA." That's the
kind of America Tony remembers … one where the sacrifices of our military are
honored with patriotism that seems passé in today's political climate.

    Other tours included going to the Philippines, Hong Kong, two ports in Japan
and dry dock in San Francisco during his two years of service.

    Tony as a senior citizen is comparable to a man of 40. His mind is sharp, his
interests are many and he loves to golf and bike ride. He was elected as an
Alderman in Boonton almost two years ago. "I am on the License and Ordinance
Committee as well as on the Economic Development Committee." Several years
ago he participated as President of BOUNCE (Boonton United Community Effort), a
group of volunteers who cleaned up public spaces near Route 287, planted gardens
around town, started Boonton's yearly "Community Day" which is held every
September and was instrumental in putting memorial bricks around the Grace Lord
Park Gazebo as a fundraiser. As he said, "It is a struggle because people came up
with lots of ideas but you need workers!" That was a good reminder that being a
'volunteer' who says, "How can I help?," is an invaluable contribution.

    He recalls seeing his mother using a washing machine with a ringer to
squeeze water out of the wet clothes.

Asked about local vendors, Tony remembered a vendor who sold vegetables out of the back of his truck, a bakery truck from Paterson, and a laundry service that picked up his father's shirts and starched and ironed them (his dad worked at the Reservoir Tavern). Tony said on the lower end of Plane Street there was also a Chinese laundry where they laundered shirts and tied them with a string. The building is still there.

Since their family didn't own a car, they shopped for clothing at Willie Frankels, Kendells Department Store (where Venturini's deli is today) and the Laurie Shop. Tony's family had chickens in the yard and his mother sewed for him a pair of pajamas from the laundered feed bags. "My mother would buy me clothes that were too big so I could grow into them. I am still not big enough," Tony laughed.

He played ball behind Jerry's field which was behind his house on Green Street. "I remember E.F. Drew would dump waste in that area." If he went there to retrieve a ball, "my sneakers would have all that stuff on them and it would smell. It is a wonder I don't light up right now." Lloyd remembers that the government provided a "Superfund" to clear up this dump which is now used as Pepe's baseball field and playground.

Tony's memories include shopping at Bednar's market, George's butcher shop, Hocker's on Cedar Street, and his Uncle Joe had Brown's market on Cedar Street and Highland Avenue.

Another staple of an era where kids were allowed to go out to play all day, was taking his flexible flyer sled and going to the top of St. Mary's cemetery. His uncle would stand on the corner of Wootton and Green watching for traffic. Tony told us, "In the 1940s there wasn't much traffic." Another great ride was to go into the woods above Sunset Lake and sleigh ride down through the woods and on to Sunset Lake which was frozen. "It was very cold but we didn't mind it."

Tony said that Boonton High School programs offered General, Academic, Scientific and College preparation. He was President of the S R A, the Student Regalian Association, during his senior year. Lloyd said that this organization was the students' government for the whole school and being its President was a very high honor. Tony found his way to the top again at Adelphi University where he majored in Business and was President of his senior class. "Who was pushing you to achieve so much?" I asked. "It just was my nature," Tony replied.

Growing up in Boonton, Tony remembers he and his friends Ron Venturini, Dick Bednar and Walter Fanning learned to play snare drum when they joined the American Legion Band. "Our uniforms were like West Point uniforms. We had head gear with a black plume and our uniforms were gray." Later, when the American Legion Band disbanded, he joined Harmony, a band that is still very much a part of Boonton life today.

Tony was too young to recall Pearl Harbor. What made a big impression was that during War II:

"I do remember blackouts, putting down the shades and a man on the street, George DeVera, who wore a metal helmet and has a big stick and a flashlight. His job was to make sure your lights were off, your shades were down and everyone was quiet. I remember they had round headlights on automobiles and the top half of the headlights were painted black so the light would not be reflected 'up.' The Air Raid siren would go off and it was scary."

I remember when I was in school in Mt. Carmel they thought a bomb would drop so we had to practice getting under the desk and putting our heads down."

As fate would have it, Tony met his future wife Monica while vacationing in Puerto Rico. They actually recognized each other from Mt. Carmel Church where Tony was an usher. They have been happily married for 33 years as of July 30.

After a career as bank manager at a Lakeland Bank in Succasunna, Tony became a tax assessor, which requires taking courses and completing a 6-hour state examination for certification. For some reason I was fascinated by this career so Tony told me the first step of an assessor is to measure the outside of the house and then to go through the home making note of the rooms.

I wondered if people complained about his assessment. "Once in a while people would be angry. You'd have to stay reasonable with them and explain – '**I don't raise taxes – the assessors put the value on the house.**' The person had the right to talk to me and sometimes they would bring something to my attention that I may have missed or I had made a mistake and I would change it."

Tony complains, "What I don't like about retirement is that I am older!" He admits to sometimes missing the 'fun' parts of his working career, but he was also clear to say he didn't "miss the times when I would say to myself at work, 'Why am I banging my head against this wall?'"

Some of the fun parts of retirement include getting senior discounts, going to the Jersey Shore during the week when it isn't crowded, the chance to ride their bikes whenever they want to, the ability to take long vacations and being able to play golf during the week.

Tony deliberately

  "stays active,

  stays positive,

  maintains a sense of humor, and

  I try not to be a worrier."

My final question, "What makes you happy every day when you wake up?" was met with an immediate response:

"When I wake up?? It is the woman in my life who is lying next to me. The best part is my wife!"

Meet Joe Strelec, a true Boontonite, friendly – appreciative - loyal – funny – reliable - generous and a little bit opinionated – great sense of humor!

I don't know when I met Joe. Maybe when our house was on the Historical Society House Tour in 2007?   Joe started talking about his website called boontonpostcards.com and we found it to be amazing with all its old photos of Boonton!   Joe attended the Senior Center when Lloyd was introducing his book, "Artistry of Bob Bogue." When he found a great photo of Lloyd's father's store on Main Street called "Royal Scarlet," he made sure to give Lloyd a copy.

Joe is friendly!

A special memory for him was getting a gift of underwear. "When you know somebody doesn't have anything and you get a gift from them it is a treasure!"

Joe is appreciative.

When Joe was 2 years old he got pneumonia. In a pre-penicillan era, that could have been fatal. "I had transfusions right from my father to me" and Joe believed that saved his life. One of seven children born during the 1930s, Joe remembers his siblings gathering around the big potbelly stove in the living room trying to get dressed by the heat of the stove. Joe has been happily married for 55 years and he held a job at Norda (the perfume maker) for 50 years! That's another Boonton trait –

Joe is loyal.

Joe recalls that Boonton was an enjoyable place in which to grow up. He learned to play a bugle and marched in the American Legion Band for several years.

He admitted he would sneak into the State Theater by the back door once in a while if he didn't have 10 cents.   Sometimes when he was very young, the temptation to take a cake that was being delivered at 7 a.m. and left in front of the A&P was overwhelming.   But he made up for it by becoming an altar boy at Mt. Carmel Catholic Church.

Joe is funny.

He enjoyed skating at Sunset Lake, hiking in the Tourne, swimming at the Basin and - when it snowed - he would tell his friends "to bring a couple of gallons of water so we could ice the hill on Lincoln Street so we could toboggan. Oh, that thing could fly!!!!"

By 16 he had dropped out of school to help support his family and he worked at the Pocketbook Factory in the shipping department.   As a teenager he was always available to "set pins" at the Elks or Johnny's Tavern because 'bowling' was an activity everyone enjoyed.

Joe was born in the mid-30s so was too young for WWII but his dad - a father of 7 children - was drafted and served in the Navy during WWII.   He remembers when the windows had to be covered with blankets and the air raid wardens checked each house to be sure no light from the house showed outside.

Joe is reliable.

Joe told me when they put in Route 287 "it definitely destroyed the character of lower Main Street."   "And selling Sunset Lake was Boonton's disaster."

Joe is opinionated! "Joe," I said, "What is the worst part of being a senior citizen?" Joe: *"It's boring!'*

"Joe," I said, "What's the best part of being a senior citizen?
Joe: *"Social Security!"*

"Joe," I said, "Can you share some words of wisdom with the next generation?"
Joe: *"LOVE MANY   TRUST FEW –*
AND LEARN TO PADDLE YOUR OWN CANOE"

Joe, your sense of humor and ready smile are your best assets!

SCERBO, LUCILE (HOPKINS) -   Interview 02/04/10 by Terry Charlton

Anyone studying "The History of Boonton 101" must be familiar with the following family histories: Hopkins, Dunn, and Scerbo. And Lucille boasts all three!

CHARLES HOPKINS

Her grandfather was Charles Hopkins. He was awarded the Medal of Honor for his bravery in the Civil War. The plaque reads: "Distinguished conduct in action at the Battle of Gaines Mills Virginia June 27, 1862 when he voluntarily carried a wounded comrade under heavy fire to a place of safety and though, twice wounded in the act, he continued in action until again severely wounded."

Charles Hopkins has his own monument at Town Hall.

Lucille said: "My grandfather took a wagon and transported the runaway slaves from the Boonton Underground Railroad Hotel to Butler, NJ."

Left: Underground Railroad Hotel was owned by Nathan Hopkins, Charles' dad.

After the war in 1865, the last of the prison camp inmates were marched to the railroad to await transportation to freedom. Only 24 were left behind, considered too hopelessly ill. One of that 24 was Charles Hopkins who crawled through the hospital and dragged his gangrenous legs across the frozen ground toward the railroad tracks.

DUNN FAMILY

Lucille's Aunt Helen wrote the Boonton High School song. Lucille's grandfather Dunn was in the Harmony Fire Department for 50 years, and her Uncle Jack was Boonton's Chief of Police. Three of Lucille's aunts became Dominican Sisters of Caldwell.

Lucille's mother's sister became Mother M. Joseph, O.P., and the head of the Dominican Order in New Jersey, who was the founder of Caldwell College.

AL SCERBO – Lucille's husband

Al Scerbo was in the Pacific in the 6th Marine division and was assigned to amphibian tanks. The Marines were his pride and joy and he was an active member of the VFW and he was Post Commander of the American Legion.

Al's father owned "Scerbo Pontiac," which was originally located on Boonton Avenue. After returning from the Marines, Al joined his father in business and they changed the car dealership location to Route 46.

Al was also a distinguished town elected official

- Alderman
- Boonton's Mayor for 6 years,
- Freeholder for 13 years and
- County Clerk for 10 years.

Al Scerbo headed the annual Memorial Day ceremony for many years where the names of the Boonton soldiers who died from World War I to the present date are read aloud and honored.

LUCILLE SCERBO

"I instituted a gym program at Mt. Carmel grammar school," Lucille said, "and I worked in it for 10 years." With donated equipment from Tony Marcello and others, they set up a program for boys and girls at the school. They competed in the 'small school' meets with local public schools and she remembers they even won trophies several times.

With such an illustrious family heritage, I anticipated that the balance of our interview would be a little low key. HA!!

Lucille began her story by telling me "there were 8 of us." Eileen, Charles, Gerald, Jody, Dolores, Edwin, Lucille, John (nicknamed "Birdie"). Her brothers were all very athletic and Jody and Birdie made All State and All County in football. Gerald was a track man and eventually became Superintendent of Northern Highlands Regional High in Allendale, NJ.

When she was about 16, her 23 year old brother Jody was killed. It was during World War II and he was assigned to the 101st Airborne as a paratrooper. He died in the Battle of the Bulge and was buried in Luxemburg. Because Lucille's mother suffered with heart problems, the family doctor, Dr. Griscom, came up to the house when the military telegram was going to be delivered. As soon as the doctor walked in, her mother knew something was wrong and said, "What is the matter with Jody?"

Lucille's dad worked as a foreman at a Ryerson Steel Mill in Bayonne, NJ and he commuted by train leaving home at 6 a.m. each morning and returning at 8 p.m. each night. In addition to that, he was a loving father and she remembers he got her a complete cowgirl outfit (from "Santa") when she was a little girl. Another time both of her sisters got doll houses and she got her heart's desire, a printing press. He was Lucille's role model for his devotion and love for his family.

I opened Pandora's Box when I asked Lucille, "Do you remember ever being sick as a child?" I was stunned by her reply.

"Oh yes. When I was 12 years old I had St. Vitus's dance. It developed after having rheumatic fever.

From doing some research I learned that rheumatic fever is an inflammatory disease, common in children between 5 and 15; it develops from strep throat or scarlet fever. It could involve the heart, joints, skin and brain and can result in St. Vitus's dance. St. Vitus's dance is characterized by involuntary muscular movements of the face and extremities as a result of an acute disturbance of the central nervous system. There is no specific treatment for this disease but eventually the symptoms disappear, but have been known to recur after several months.

"My father used to lie down on my body just to keep me from jumping all over the place when I first got it. And they gave me a baby bottle for nourishment because I couldn't hold anything."

"They didn't expect me to live through my teens," Lucille said. "They thought I would be a cardiac case." I said, "Well you sure fooled them!!!!"

Although she totally recovered within a year, her physical condition was fragile. The family consensus was to send Lucille to Mt. St. Dominic Academy in Caldwell, NJ where she boarded on weekdays so as to encourage her return to full health.

When we got to reminiscing, Lucille and I laughed over the shared memory about hanging "tinsel" on the Christmas tree. "First you carefully placed one strand of tinsel on at a time and then all of a sudden you'd throw it all on." We both remembered that an Irish Sunday tradition was serving a big roast leg of lamb for dinner. When they had a thunderstorm, Lucille's mother used to light "blessed candles" and they would all kneel down and say a prayer.

To my question, were you permitted to walk around town? "Well sure you could. That was the most beautiful part of growing up in Boonton. You weren't afraid to walk around town. You knew everybody and they knew you and if you were doing something wrong, they'd let your mom know about it."

How about sleigh riding? She recalled with awe, "My brother went down Spruce Street! Now that's a big run -- from the top all the way down by the railroad. We didn't have the kind of traffic we have now."

Did I forget to mention Al and Lucille adopted two daughters through Catholic Charities? Her own daughters were 7 and 8 at the time, and Maria and Jennie were 9 and 7. Their family of origin was Cuban and the girls' mother and father were able to come to America four years later and they formed a loving 'extended family' relationship with the Scerbos.

I couldn't help but point out to Lucille that having four girls so close in age was the equivalent of having a set of quadruplets to bring up! Characteristically, she responded, "It was wonderful! I got so much more than I gave. And they are still my girls."

Al doted on their one granddaughter who is presently attending Boston University. "Talk about my joy!" Lucille said, "I just adore her."

"How long ago did your husband Al die?" I ask softly. "Monday it was one year," she replied just as softly.

"But I feel his presence in the house."

Lloyd added, "The Town misses Al."

Thank you," she said.

WERNER, PAUL -

Paul's dad needed a job in the hosiery industry and brought his family from Reading, Pennsylvania to Boonton in 1935 so he could work at Van Raalte, a silk manufacturer. Paul was just an infant at the time and he grew up on Boonton Avenue. A highlight memory of his childhood was the red 'quarantine' sign on his house because he had contracted measles, mumps and chicken pox over a 6 week period.

Be assured, these childhood diseases did not stunt Paul's growth as he is well over 6 feet and he can't remember a time when he wasn't the tallest child in the class. "No matter what I wore on Halloween, everyone knew who I was!"

As a very small boy, he remembers going to visit grandma in Reading. PA and watching the trolley cars in front of grandma's house. In the winter, the track 'sweepers' would be used and "I found that fascinating." If that weren't excitement enough, at 4 p.m. when the people got out of work, the trolleys would be lined up all the way down the block ready to take the people home. So, because of his fascination with all things electric, when Paul was only 5 years old his uncle spent $35 to buy him a Lionel train set (which he still proudly owns 70 years later). This gift was outlandishly expensive in an era when a man earning $45 salary per week would be paid very well! I commented to Paul, "What a perfect gift for a little boy," to which he responded, "And even for a big kid! You know the saying – 'The only thing that separates men from boys is the size and cost of their toys.'"

Asked where he liked to play, Paul recalled, "In the good old days you would leave the house in the morning, come home for lunch and disappear again." He loved Saturday matinees at the State Theater, skating or swimming at Hillary's Pond, sleigh riding ("winters were colder way back when" he believes), climbing up Indian Rock, going up to the Water Tower on Sheep Hill and playing pickup games of baseball. He even had his own glove.

Paul would have been about 10 years old when the Japanese surrendered and he tells this story: "It was so exciting. I remember marching up and down Main Street all night long carrying a fuzi (phonetic)."

When asked about what radio programs he enjoyed, Paul remembered "Tennessee Jed" – (then … making a shooting noise) – "Got him dead center!"

"Tennessee Jed was a radio program that ran from 1945- 1947. It was an action-packed juvenile western serial with a trusty horse called Smoky. Tennessee Jed became a White House agent working directly for the president to stomp out all evil.

Paul distinctly recalls one Sunday in 1941 when he almost 7, he was listening to the Moylan Sisters when the program was interrupted to announce that the Japanese bombed Pearl Harbor. "I knew that meant war."

We did some research and learned that the Moylan sisters (ages 5 and 7) were first featured on the radio program: The Horn and Hardart Children's Hour, and were soon given their own 15-minute network radio program.

"I remember around 1952 when they tore up Main Street, took out the trolley tracks and repaved it. Zagara's market was affected by the Main Street closing, which went on for several weeks. In his frustration he went out and planted a Victory garden in the middle of the middle of the street." Paul believes Main Street was made 18 inches wider on each side!

When Newberry's new location on Main Street and Boonton Avenue was being constructed, Paul remembers they dug a deep hole and it filled with water. When he later worked in Newberry's he could hear the sump pump working. Boonton Avenue was originally named "Brook Street" for a reason.

Paul remembers when he volunteered in Civil Defense as a young adult, one Halloween he had a policeman assigned to his car. They spotted a group of boys in front of Bednar's Market and the policeman asked one boy, "What do you have in your pants pocket?" With that he tapped the boy's pocket and the raw eggs he had been hiding broke.

Paul served for three years in the Army and was stationed in Alaska doing "classified" work. "There was a woman behind every tree," he reminisces with a smile. "Well, that is, there weren't any trees on the Aleutian Islands."

One day he was talking to a friend on lower Main Street, when two girls wearing Boonton jackets passed by. And that's how he met Lucretia, nicknamed "Cris." After he returned from the Army, they were married and their son Paul, Jr., is now living in Pittsburgh. Sadly, when she was only 50, Cris died very suddenly from the ramifications of diabetes. I asked him how he coped with such a shocking loss. "What are you going to do? You can't change anything." He feels having a sense of humor, albeit he admits his is a little sacrilegious, is what makes a bad situation survivable. "Otherwise – life can knock you over."

A part of his career that delighted Paul was working in the radio and television department at Morristown High School and watching the 10 Watt FM radio station go to 150 Watts and stereo. "Over the years, I rewired the radio station five times. It is still in existence – Station WJSB."

Paul keeps busy as a member of the First Presbyterian Church. He has been a member of the Mountain Lakes Masonic Lodge for over 50 years. But the nicest story he told? He had found a way to fulfill his childhood dream of becoming a trolley motorman. At this point, Paul leaves the room and returns wearing his own motorman hat. He has a seasonal job driving a trolley during tourist season in Scranton, PA.

There are two things to know, he says, about trolleys. The First Law of Physics – Two objects cannot occupy the same space at the same time. And the Second Law – Things in motion stay in motion – especially when one of them weighs 300 tons.

The moral of the story?

If you pull your car in front of a trolley – the trolley is probably going to hit you.

WISWALL, FRANK & MAE (BEIERMEISTER) - Interview 02/09/10by
Terry Charlton

Mae and Frank Wiswall have a beautiful home decorated with a charming collection of Hummel figures. She is the 'Grace Kelly' and he is the 'Bob Hope' of Boonton Avenue. Frank was born in 1919 and Mae was born 14 years later. Mae is both pretty and protective of her husband.

One of Frank's stories still brings a smile to my face.

It seems Frank is one of those unfortunate kids who had a laugh that was very loud. Frank said, "I went to a movie in Chatham to see *Ghost Breakers.* There were ghosts all around – and this black servant was hiding and trembling inside a grandfather's clock." Impersonating the man's terrified high pitched voice, Frank mimicked, "**Ghost you don't scare me none!**" Frank absolutely could not control his laughter and he was asked to leave the theater.

Some people are born to laugh and Frank is one of them. My first question "Were you born in the hospital?" got this reply: "I don't know. I wasn't there at the time."

Asked about Halloween, Frank said, "We would take an ash can and prop it against the front door and then we'd ring the doorbell and run like H.E. double sticks."

His grandfather was trying to dissuade Frank and his friends from playing in an abandoned house. "So he called me aside one night and pointed to an upstairs window and said 'That's where the skull and bones lives' and he knows you kids are coming in the house." It worked. He didn't play there again.

215

When that same grandpa fell asleep in a chair and snored loud enough to be heard in the next town, Frank would "get a big hunk of that smelly cheese, put it on a long fork and I waved it below his nose."

"My mother had a singing class and they met at our house because we had a big piano and the ladies would sing LA LA LA LA. One day they were doing that and I went outside under the window and went "AW OOOOOOO" (making a wolf sound).

"I was very small. My dad's boss held out each hand and in each was a quarter – one was a dirty old quarter and the other was a nice shiny quarter. And Mr. Campe said, 'Which one do you want?' So I took both of them."

It soon became apparent I needed to learn about Boonton through Mae's memories. The third oldest of 9 children, her father was a meter reader at JCP&L. "In those days nobody got real sick. We used to play in the snow and if we didn't have gloves we'd put socks on our hands."

She remembers they had chickens and her Aunt Bessie could make wonderful dresses from the chicken feed bags that came in beautiful material and different designs. She remembers babysitting and charging 25 cents an hour. She remembers that she had to light the stove to heat the water for a bath. Also, "We couldn't go out until the dinner dishes were done and we were expected to help hang the family's laundry on the weekend."

Mae remembers a herdy gerdy man with a music grinder and a monkey. "It was so wonderful to see that monkey."

"Even as children we could walk around town. We didn't lock our doors. I used to love to sleigh ride down Spruce Street." She remembers it cost less money if you bought a ticket and sat in the balcony at the State Theater.

I asked if she volunteered and Mae said she wanted to work in the women's auxiliary of the fire department. "Your husband had to be a fireman, unless you were voted in by the others, plus you had to have a brother or father who was a fireman. I had two brothers who were firemen so that's how I got voted into the auxiliary and I am still a member."

Asked about his military career, Frank said he signed up in 1939 for the National Guard in Newark in the 102nd Cavalry believing he would be discharged in one year. After Pearl Harbor, Frank Wiswall went into the Air Force and flew as a bombardier in performing 25 missions (the maximum allowed) in Europe during World War II.

"The Germans used to have aircraft flying at the same height off to our wing – either side – radioing back to the Luftwaffe forces on the ground where our plane was heading, what our air speed was, what our altitude was – so they could get their 80 millimeter anti-aircraft guns right on us." I believe Frank told me that he earned the Distinguished Flying Cross and the Air Medal four times, three clusters. A few months ago Frank was invited to the French Consulate where he was awarded the "The French Legion of Honor."

Frank and Mae married in 1953, and were happily bringing up their four children, when their oldest son Frank, age 17, was in a fatal car accident. Mae said God had given them their son Jeff later in their marriage, and Jeff was only 4 at the time of the accident. Taking care of him kept them going. "We could have gone completely to pieces but we didn't." Then six years ago their son Tommy was in a fatal automobile accident. Two years ago Frank's daughter (who had been brought up by his wife from a previous marriage) died of cancer.

No interview with a person over 75 years old is free of stories of heartbreak and tragedy. But I was having a really hard time keeping my composure during this part of the interview. "It's a tough story," said Mae but then she assured me it brought her and Frank closer together.

Also, instead of focusing on these incredibly sad stories, Mae began to speak about their wonderful son Jeff and daughter Lynn, their grandchildren and great grandchildren.

I asked her – what brought a smile to her face not counting family or career. She said "We love the garden. We love the beach." Frank said he loved his "ham radio."

And suddenly my first impression came back. They were 'Grace Kelly' and 'Bob Hope' again. I was hoping they would sing "*True Love*" as we left the interview.

In 2007, when Lloyd had his 80th birthday my son-in-law, Lee Harris (the NYC 1010WINS radio news announcer), created a 20-minute movie about Lloyd's life which we previewed at the Darress Theater. Congressman Rodney Freylinghausen came to the party and presented Lloyd with a flag that was flown over the Capitol. Here is Rodney Frelyinghausen and Mayor Wikelski making fun of the spats worn by Rev. Harold Johnson.

Photo by Warren Westura

In January 2009, Lloyd self-published a book about his friend's artwork.
He called it: THE ARTISTRY OF BOB BOGUE. Here's our celebration party photo!

Made in the USA
Charleston, SC
27 December 2010